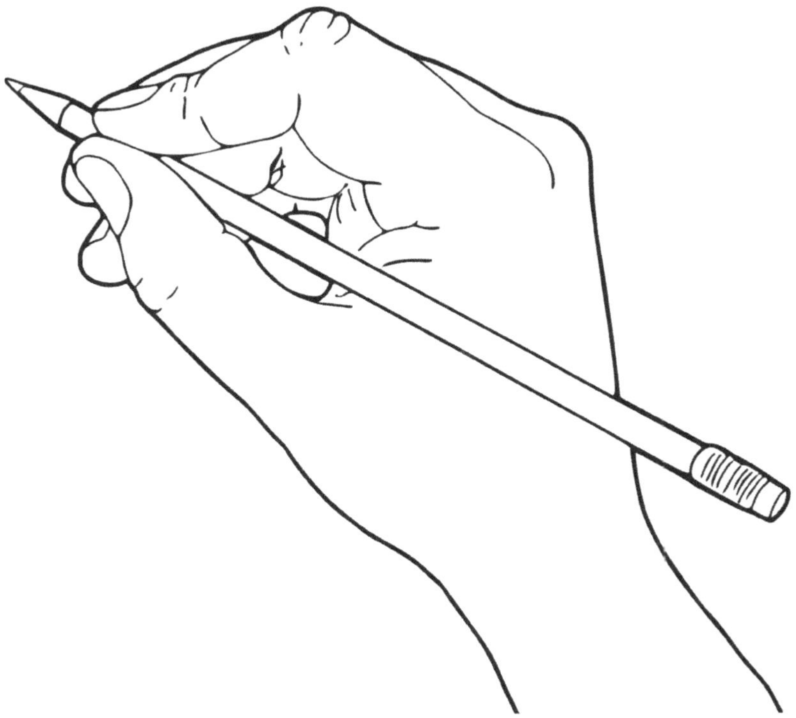

This Notebook belongs to:

____

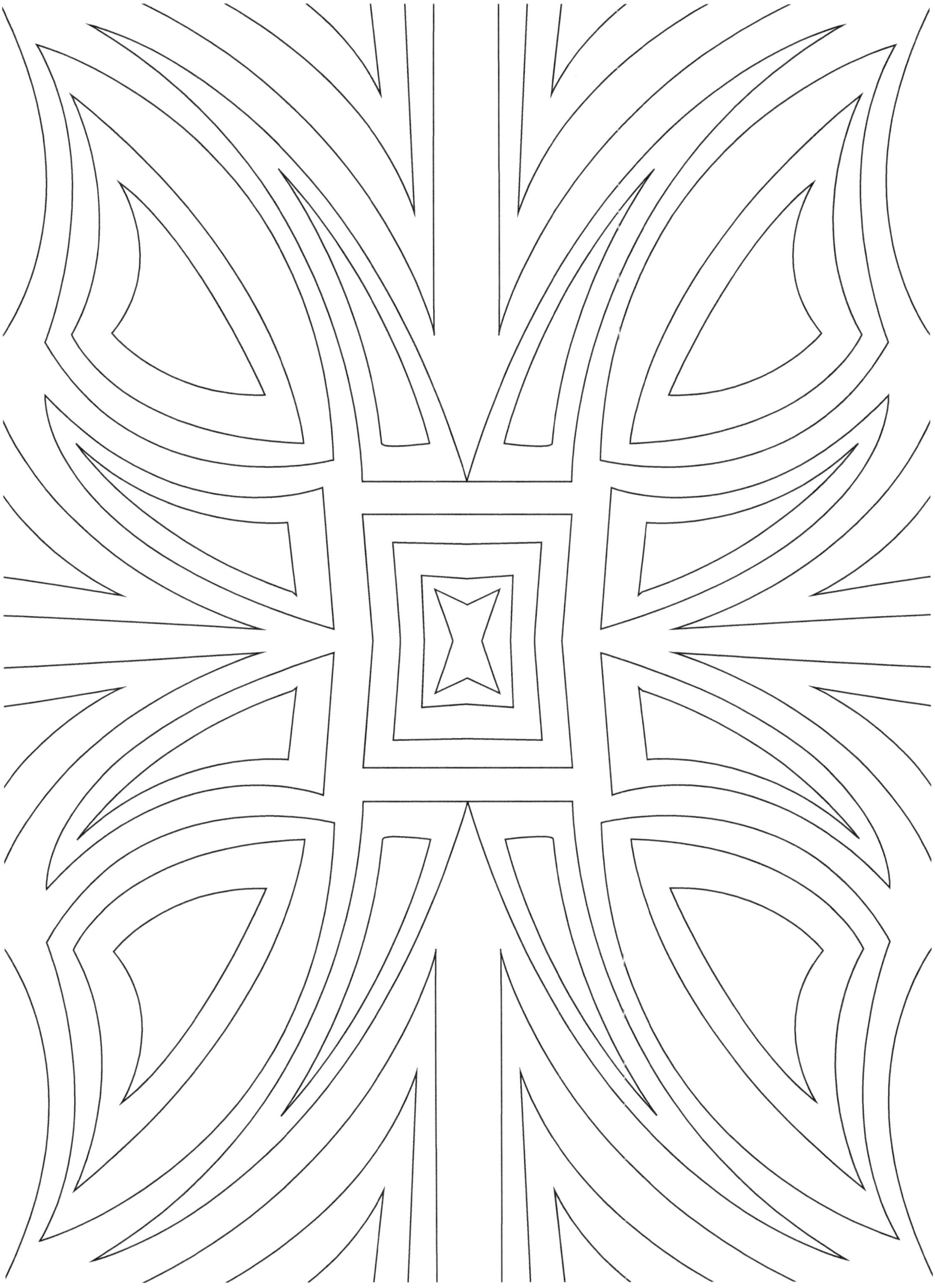

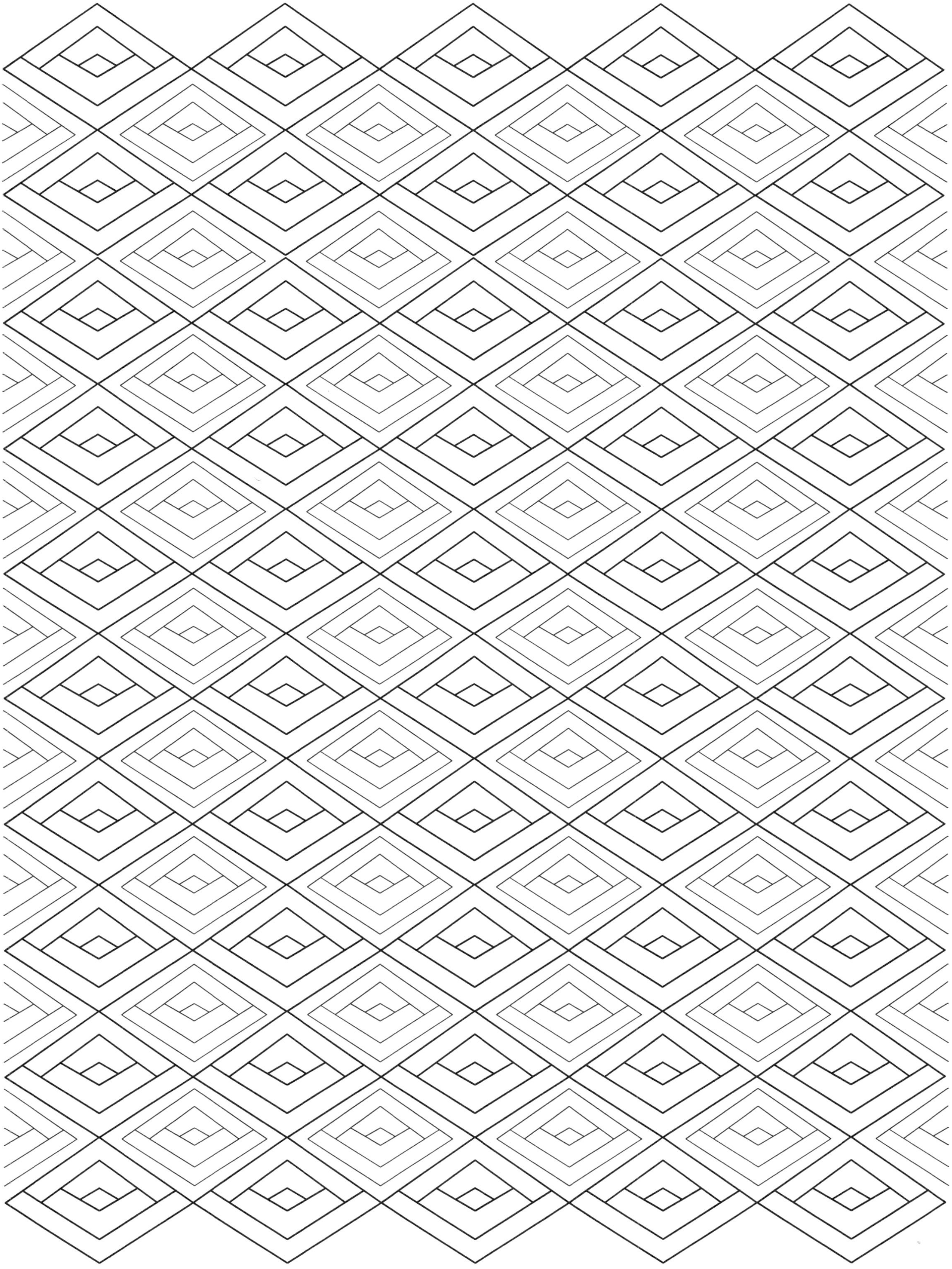

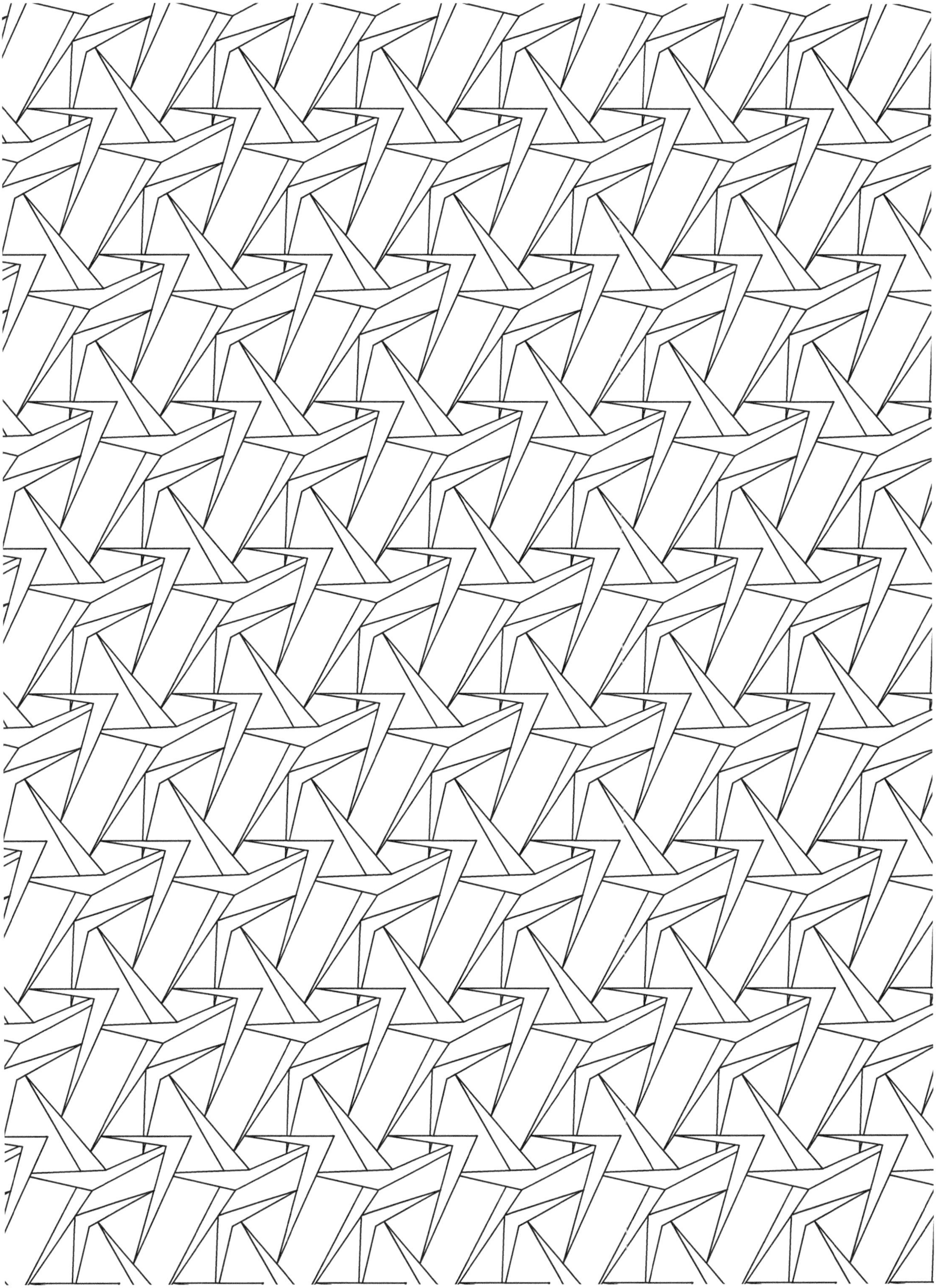

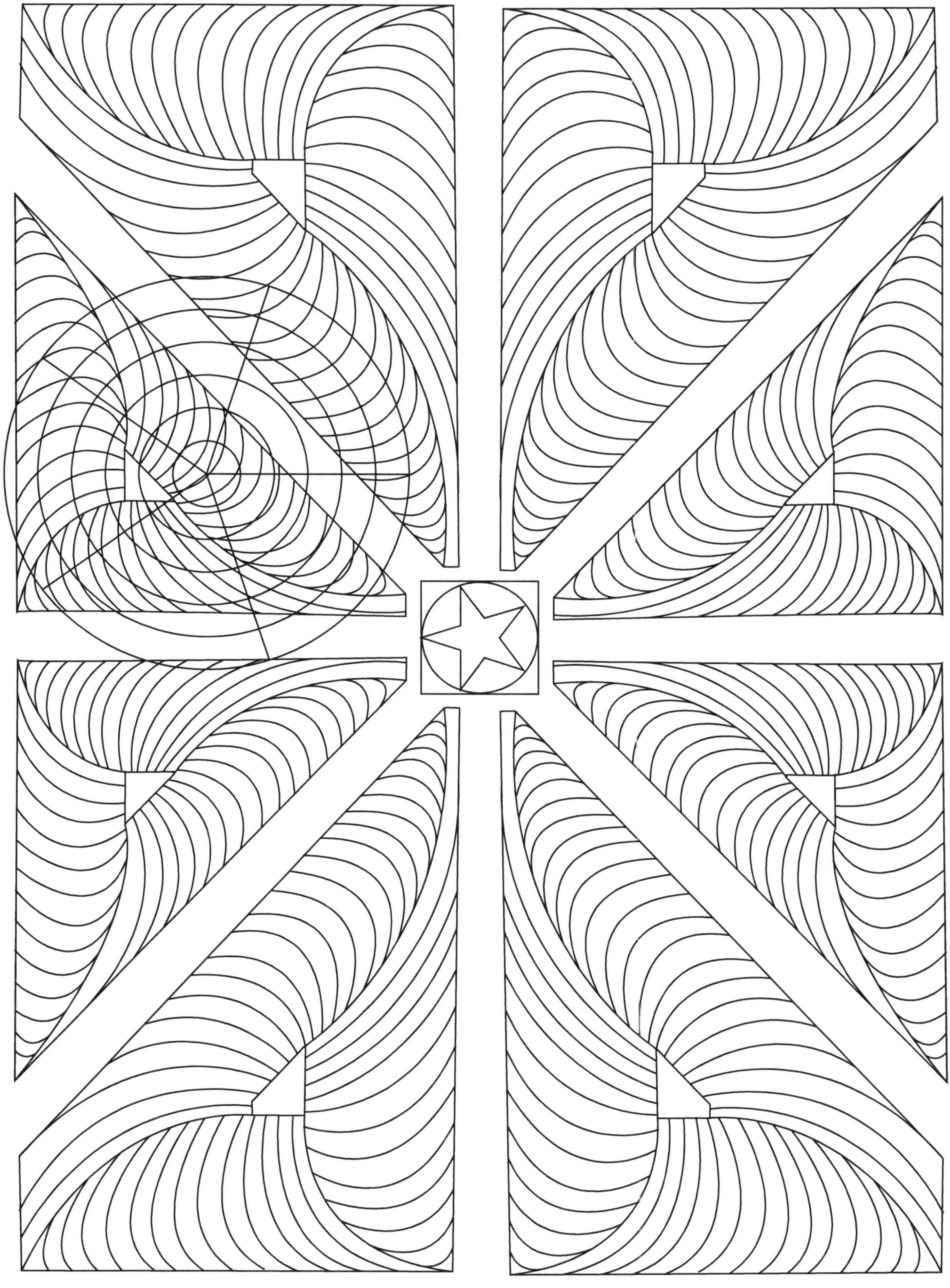

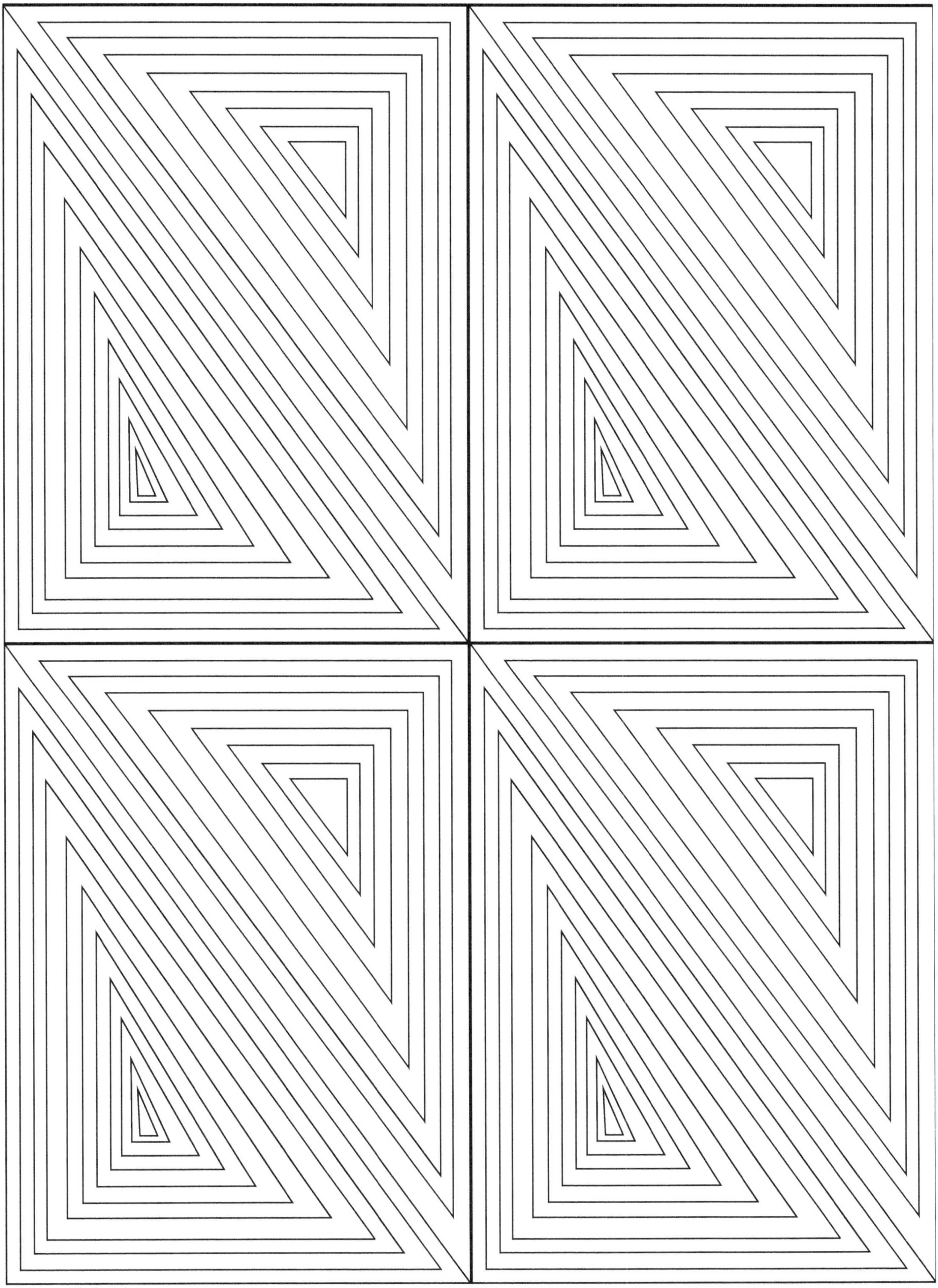

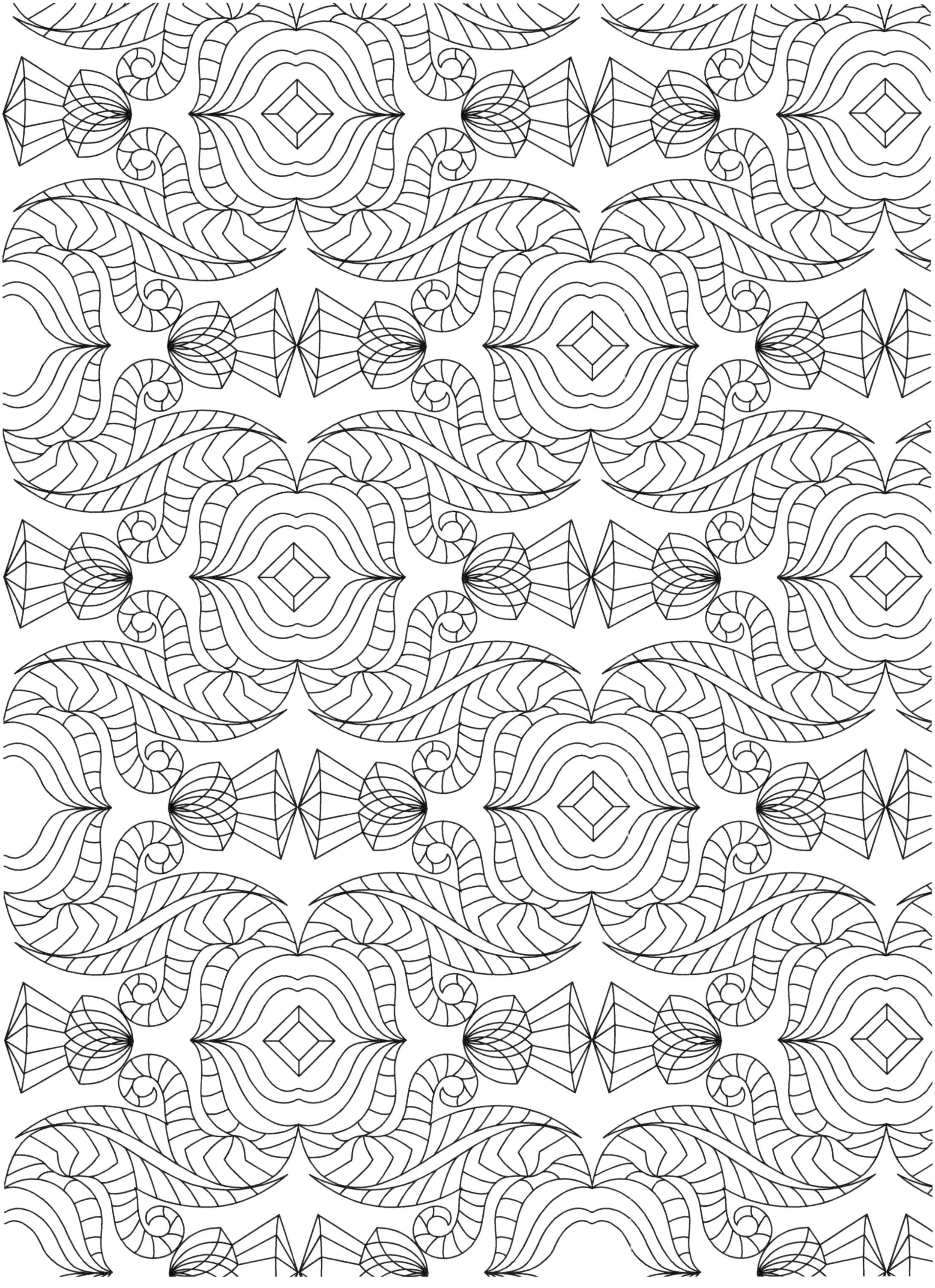

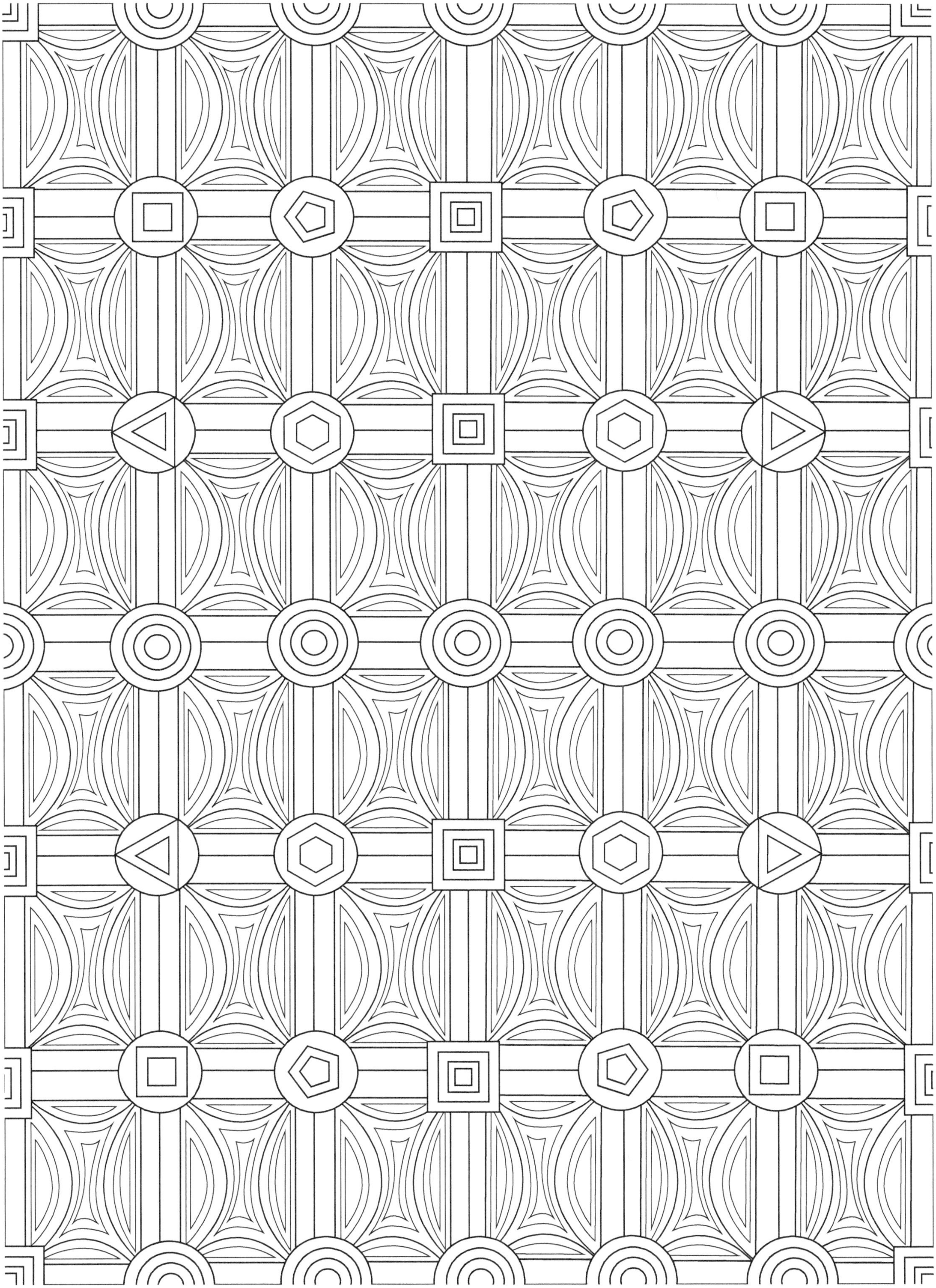

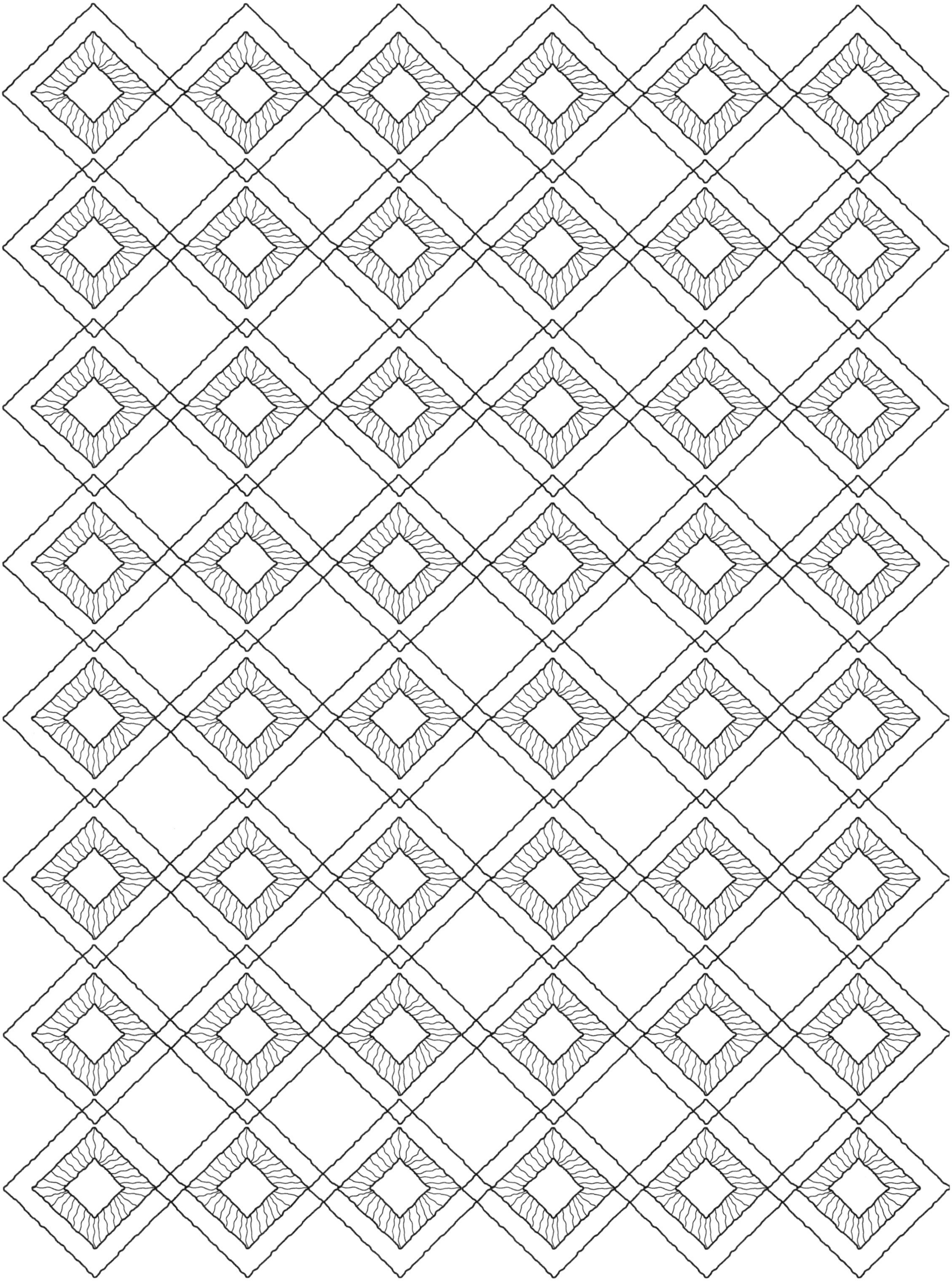

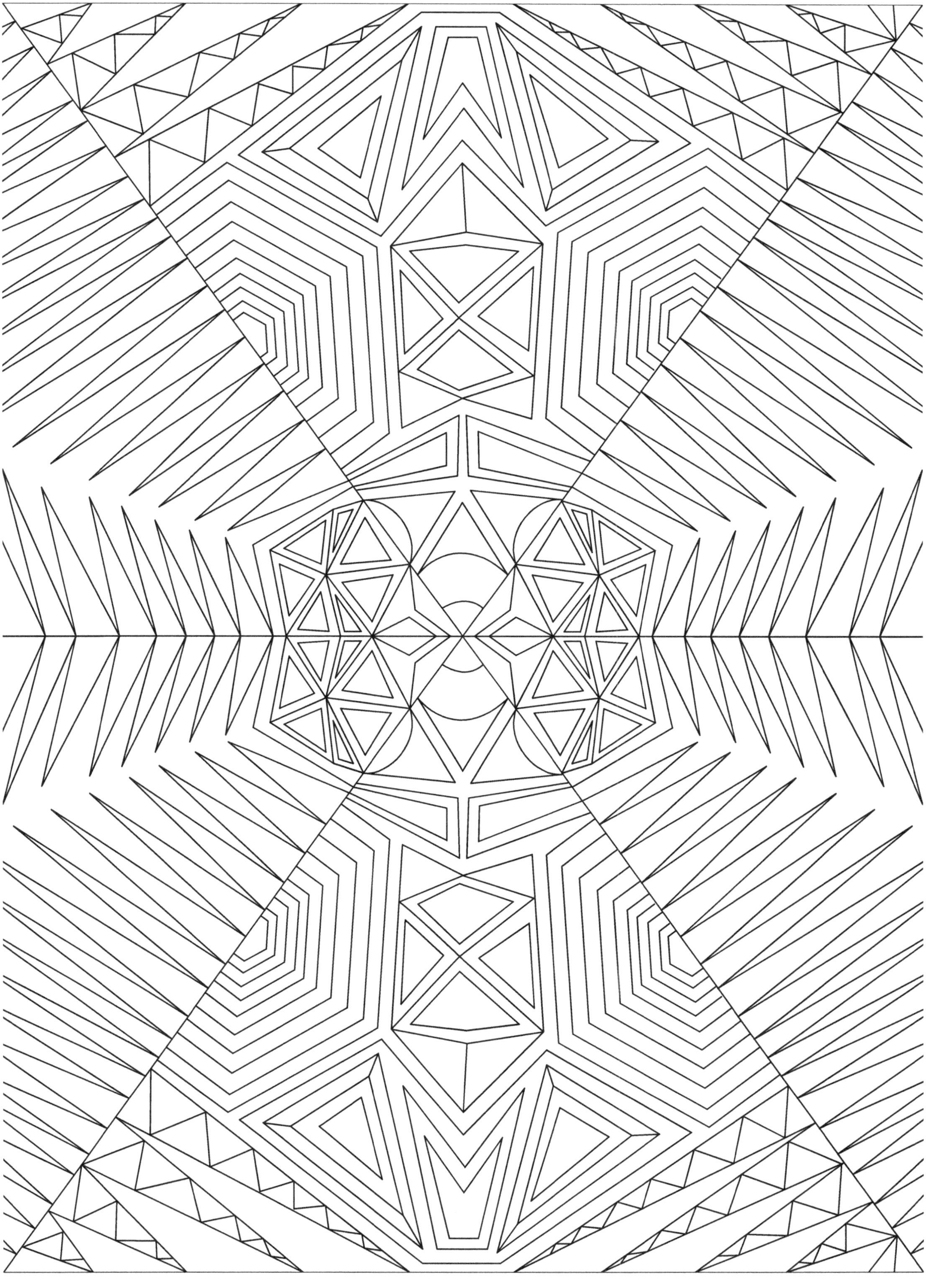

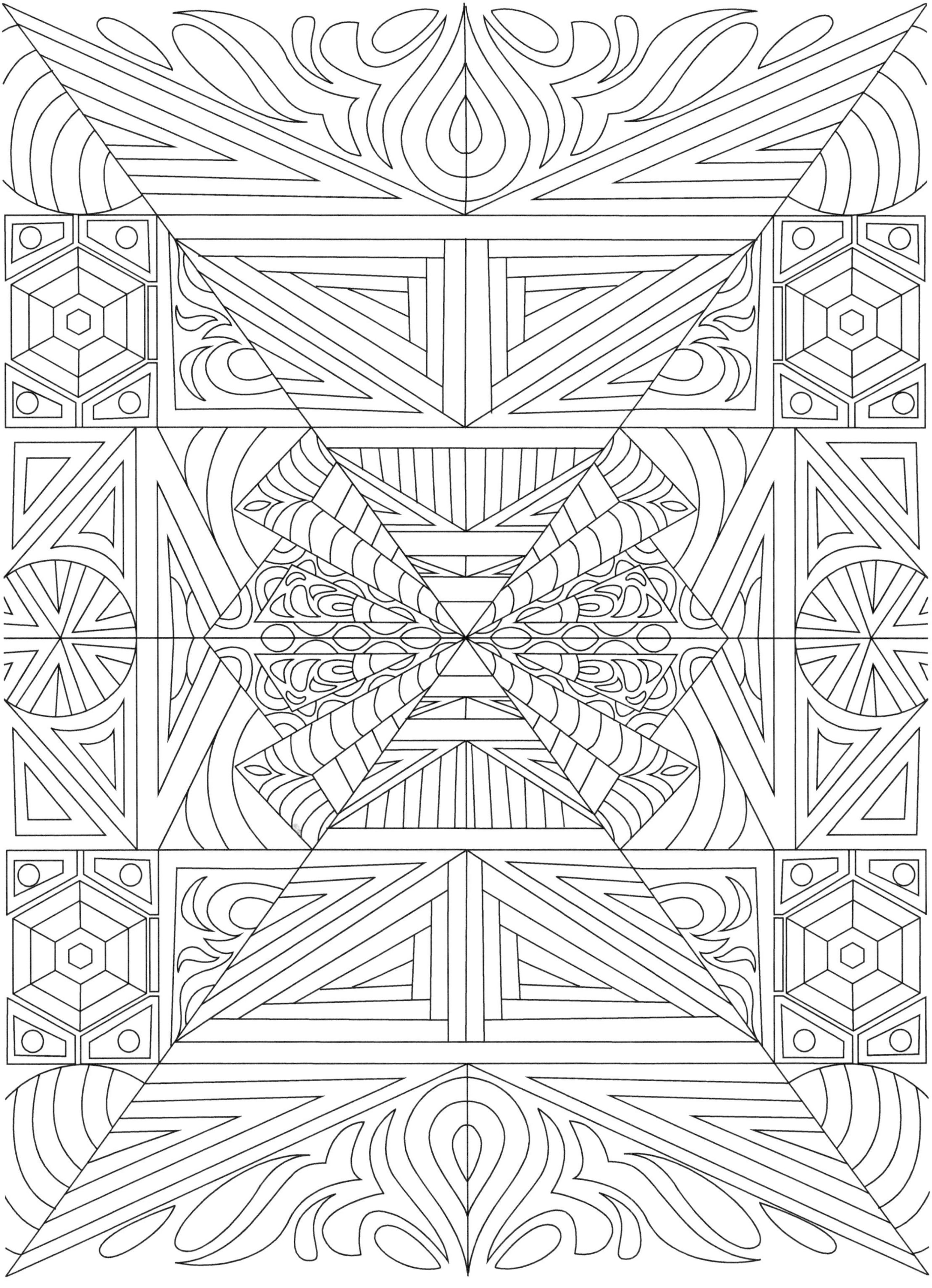

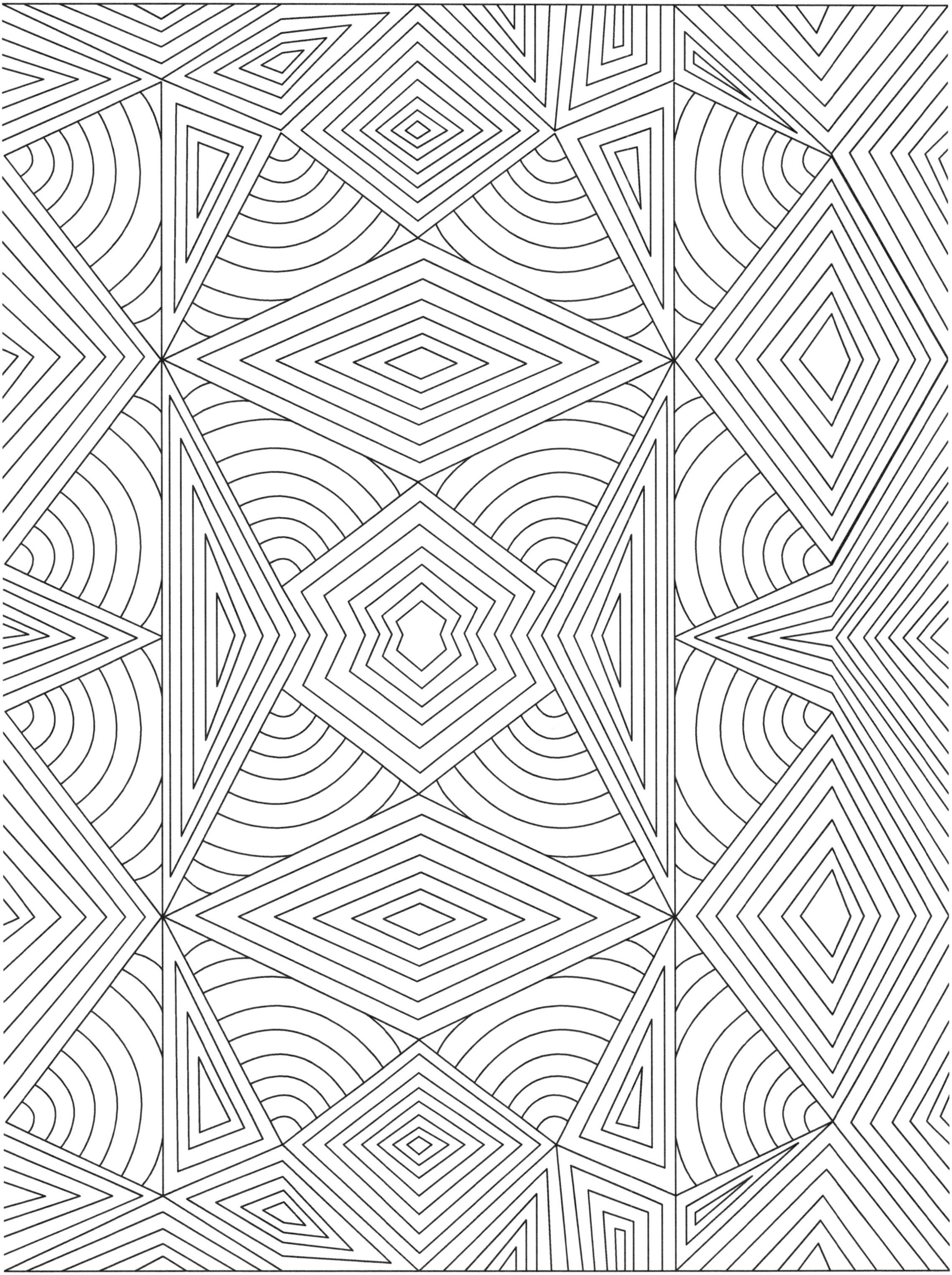

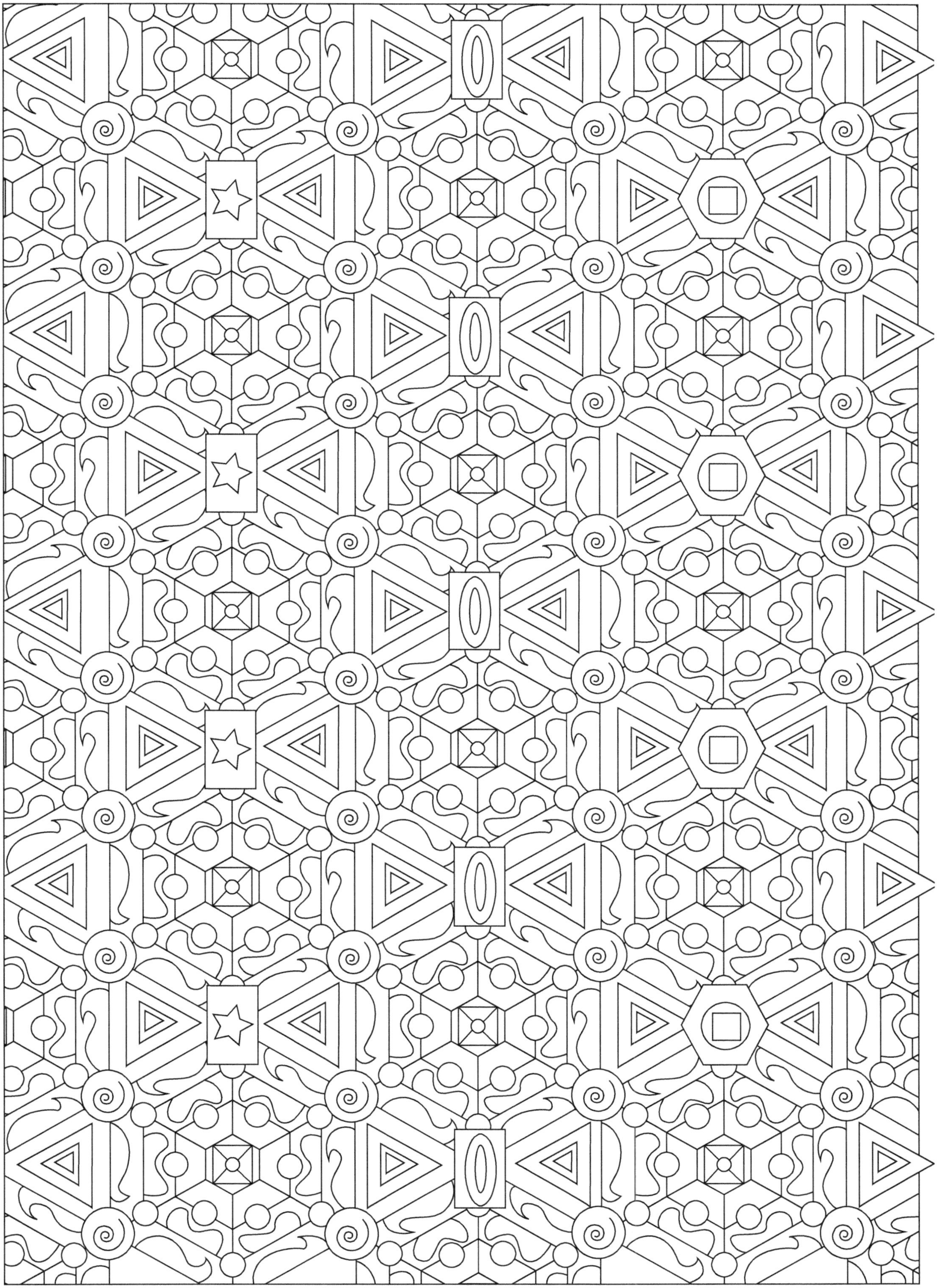

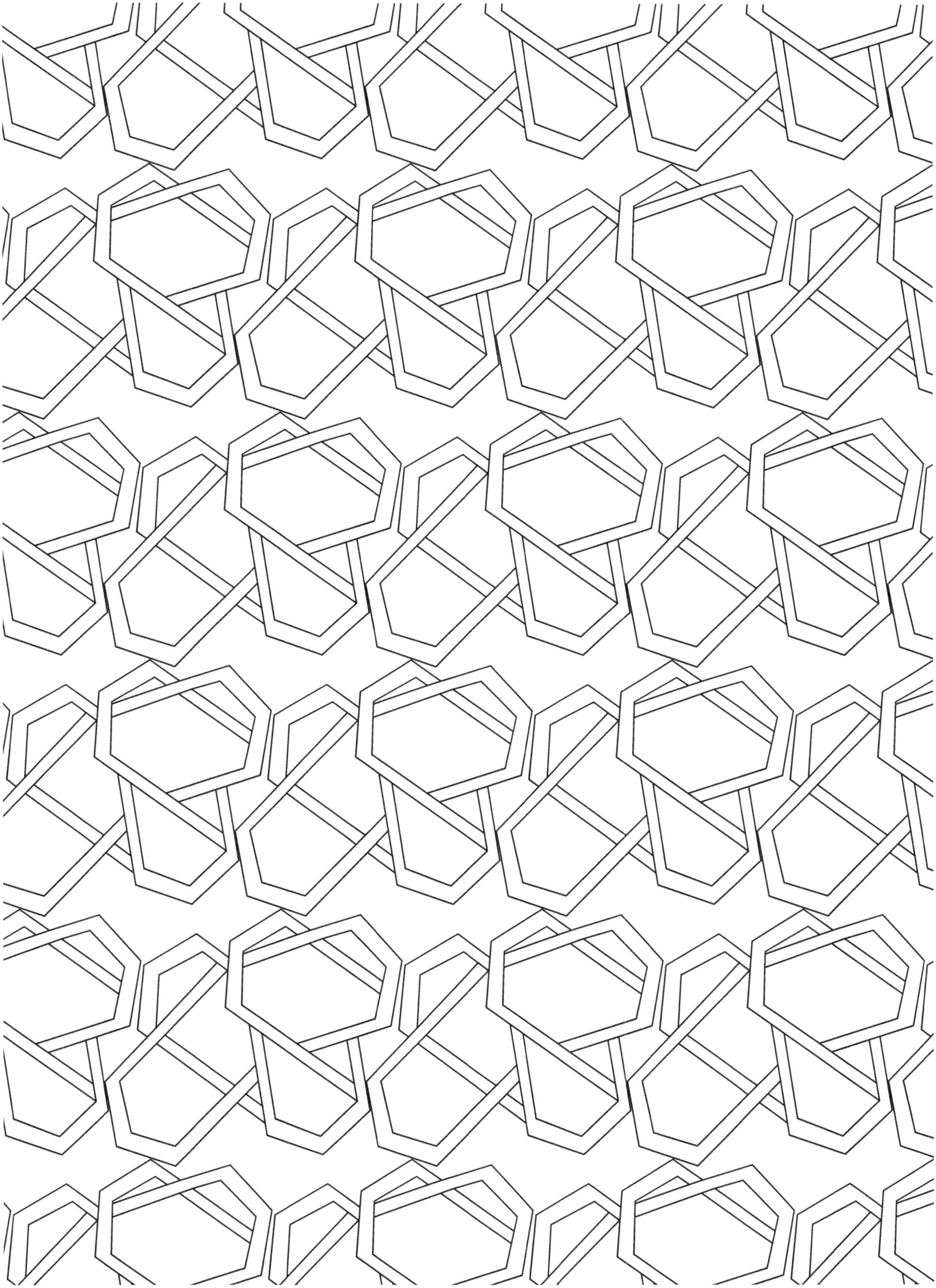

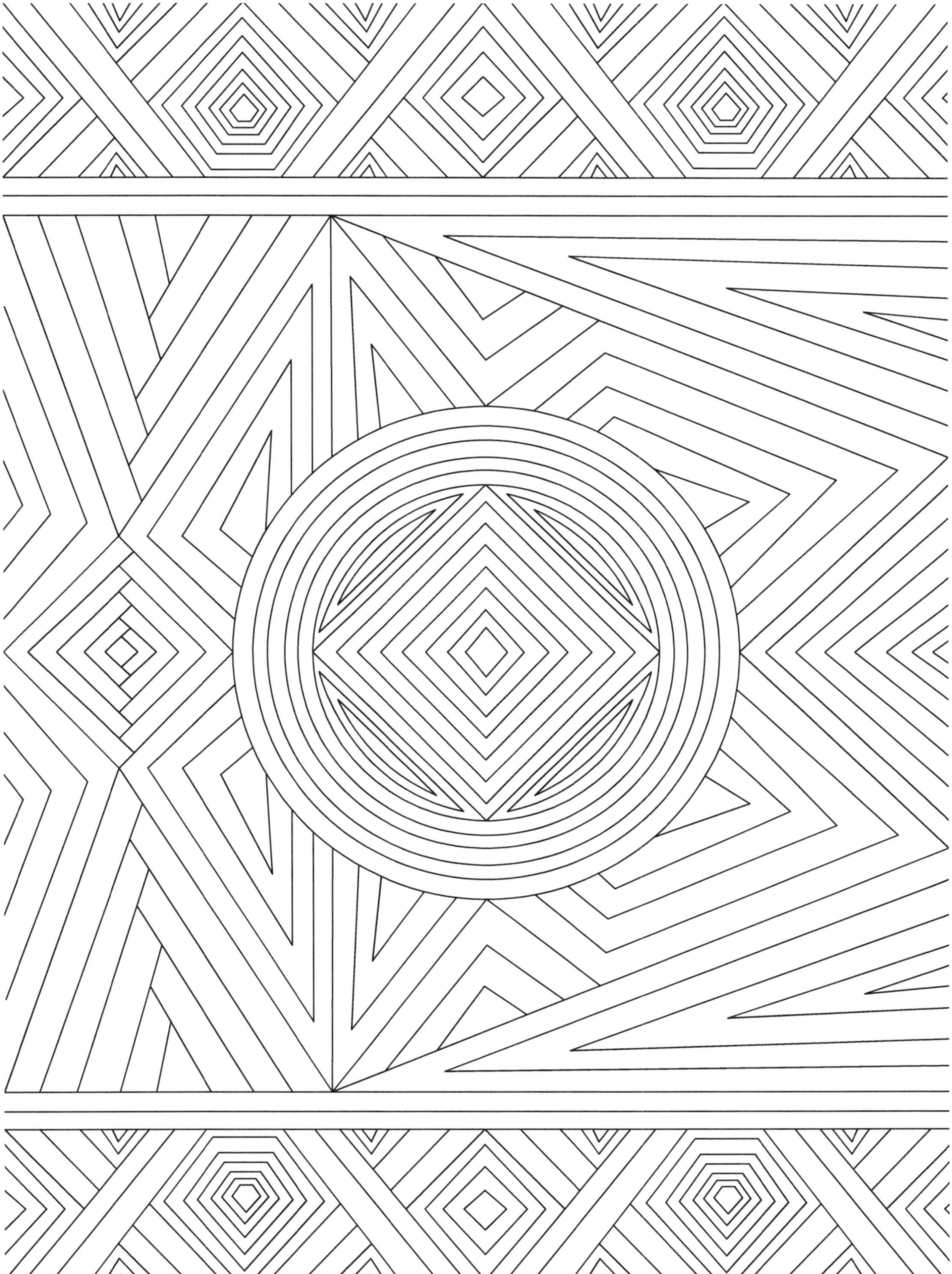

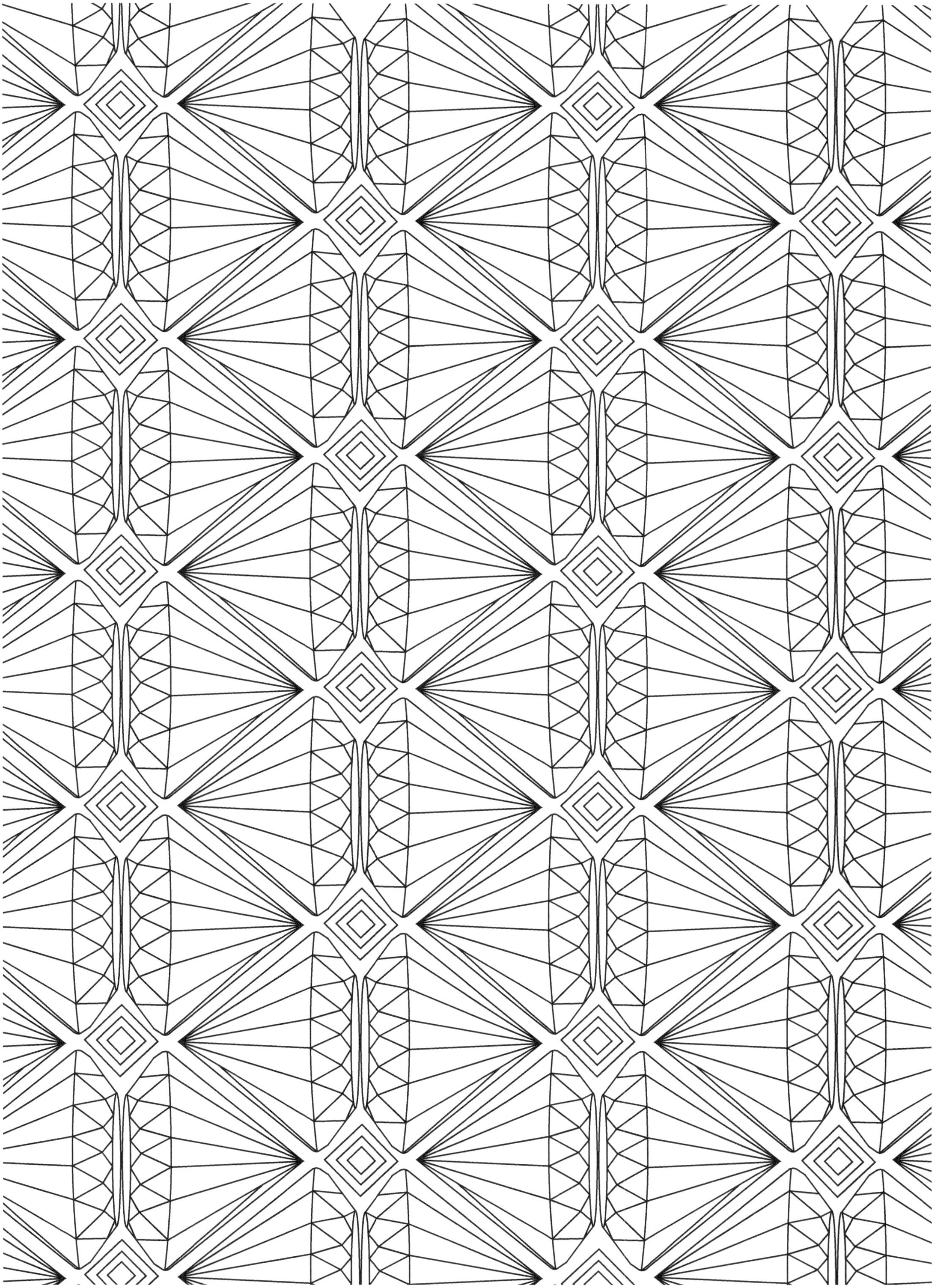

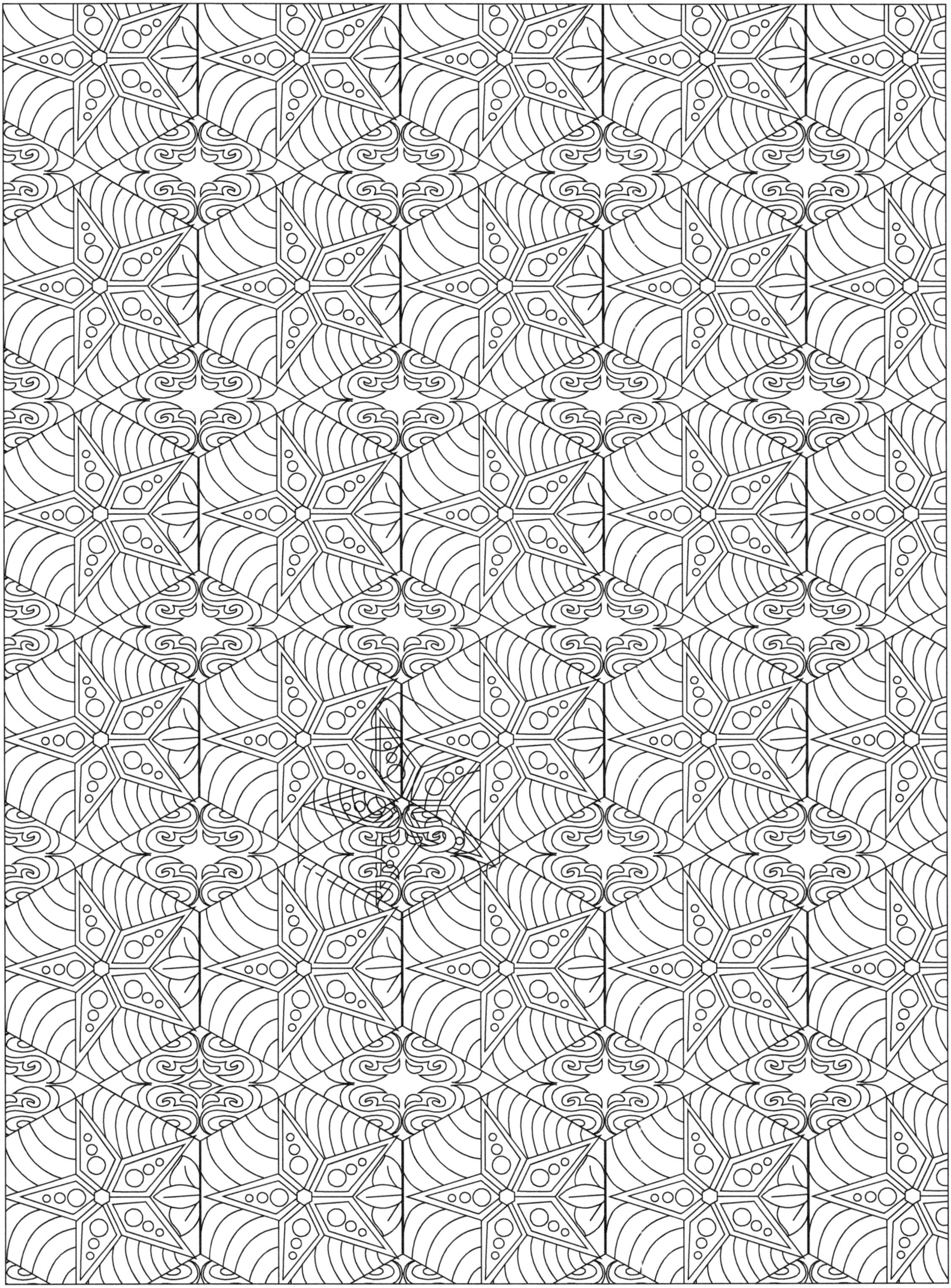

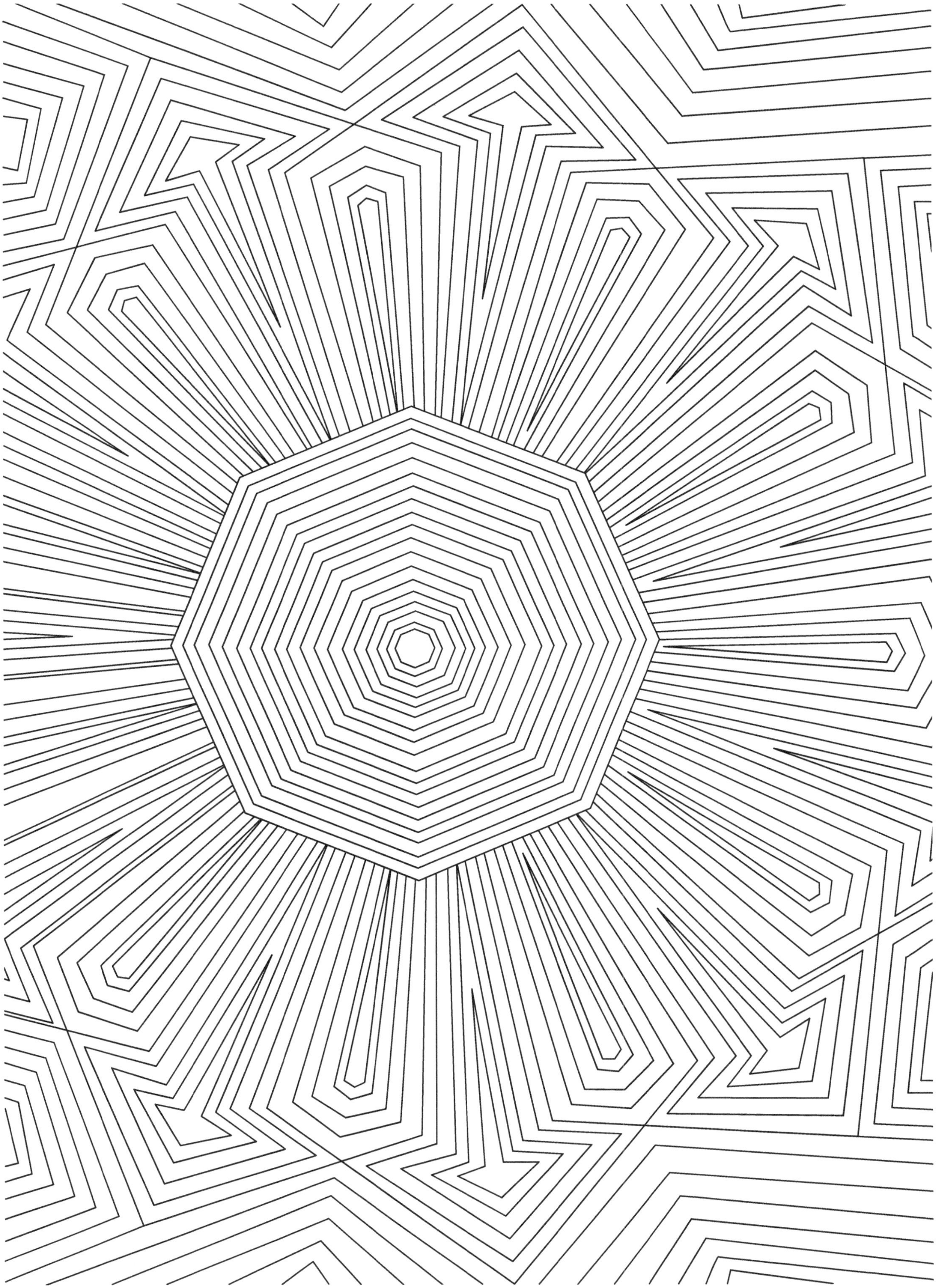

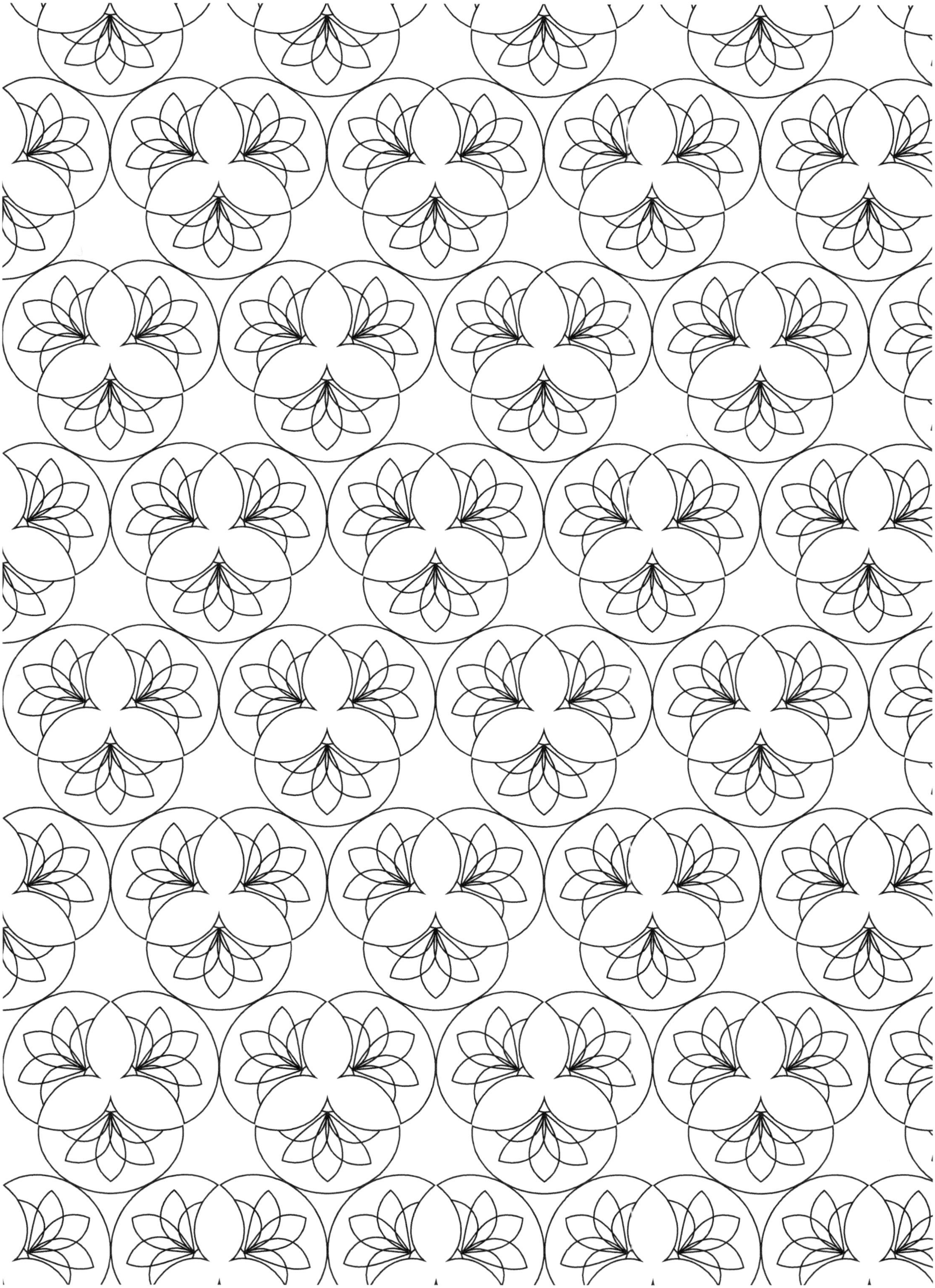

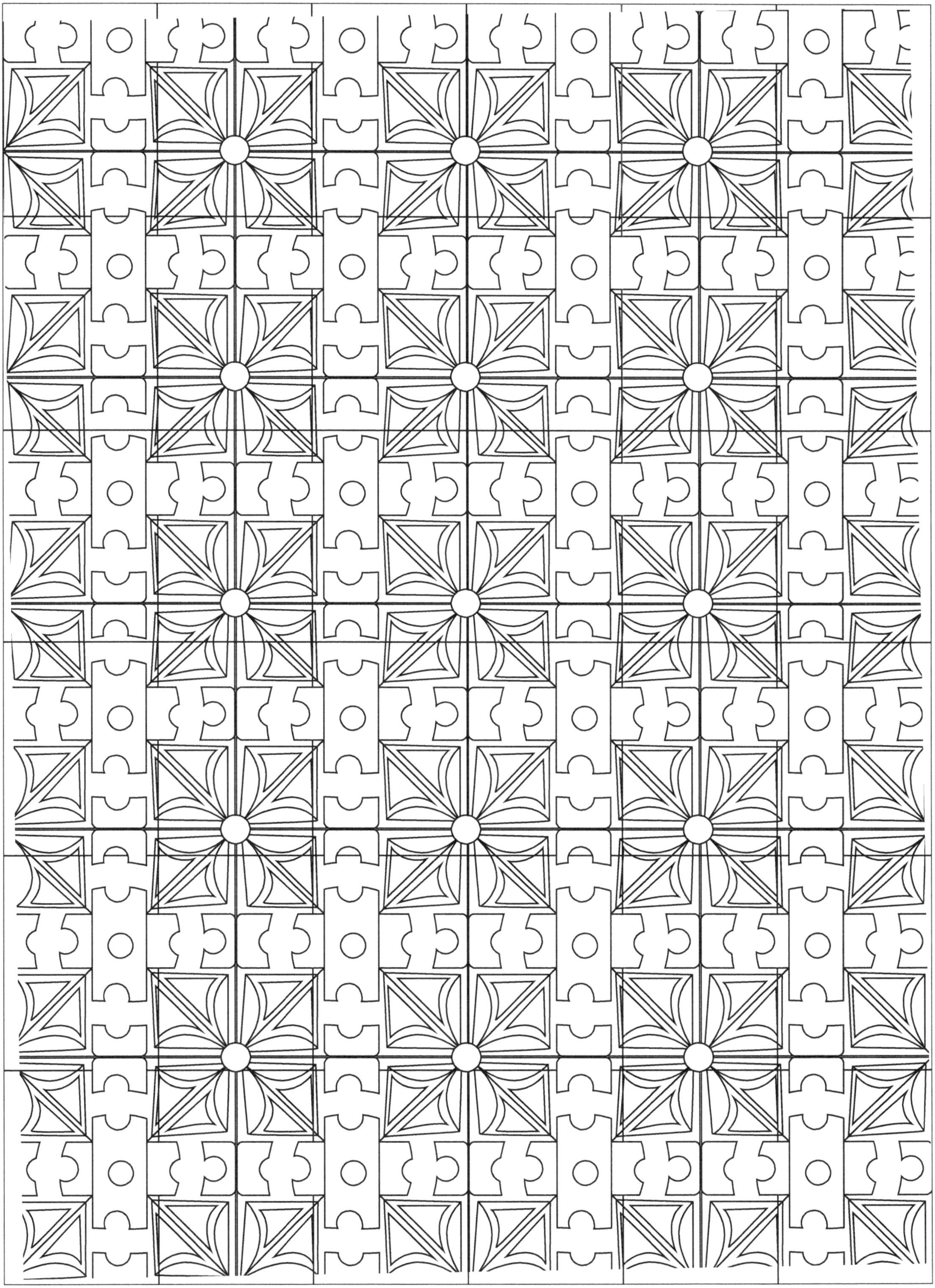

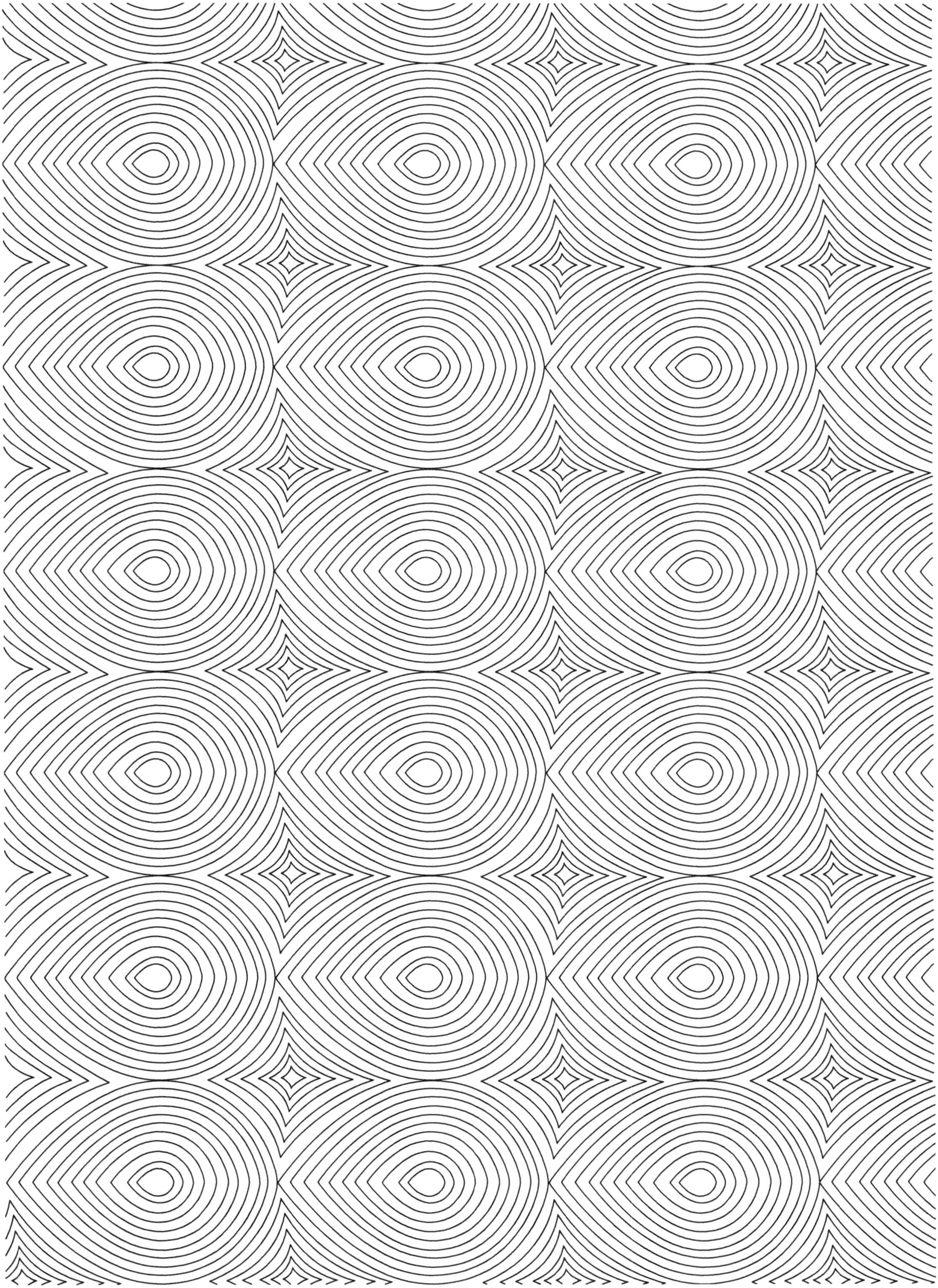

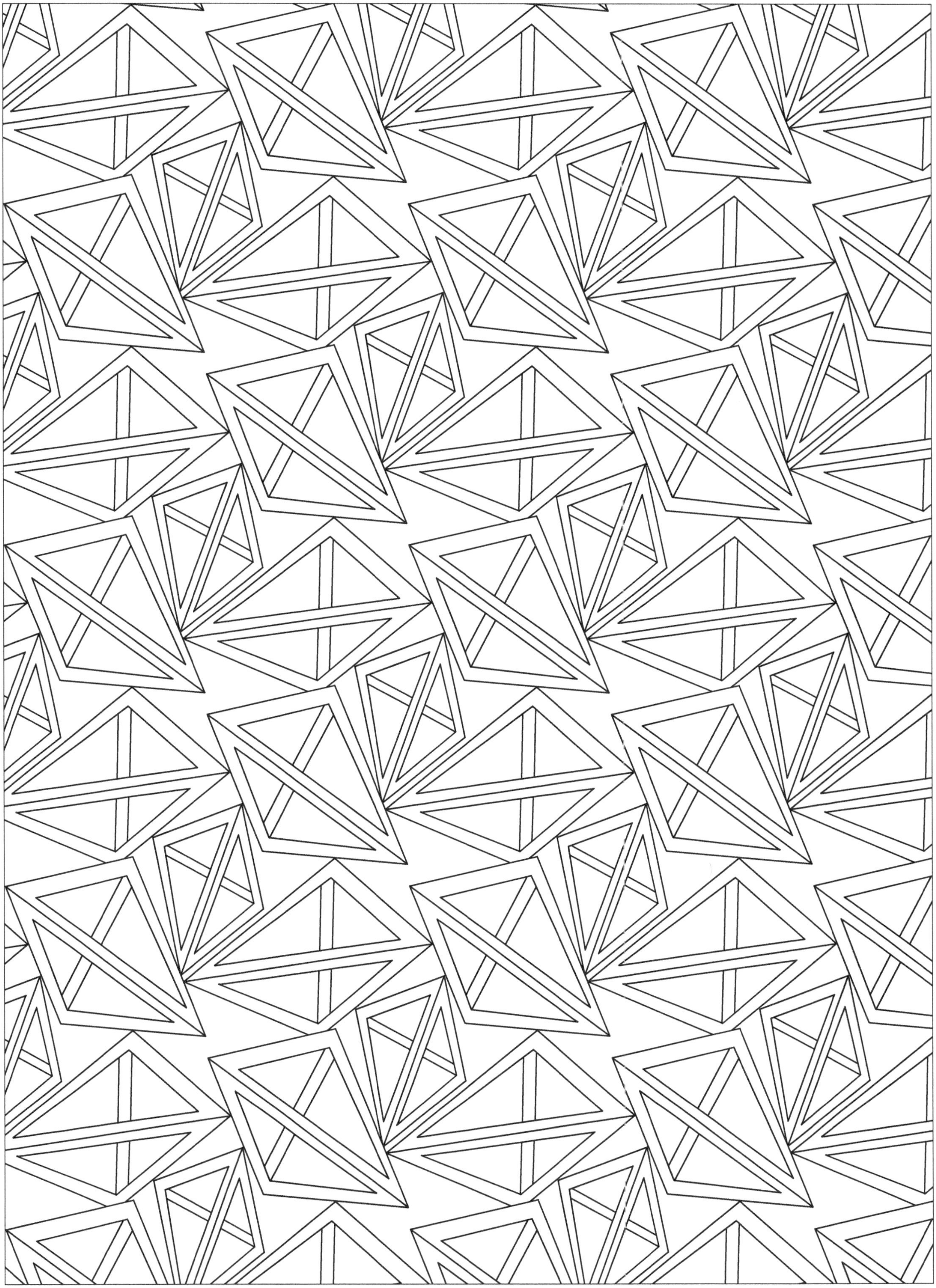

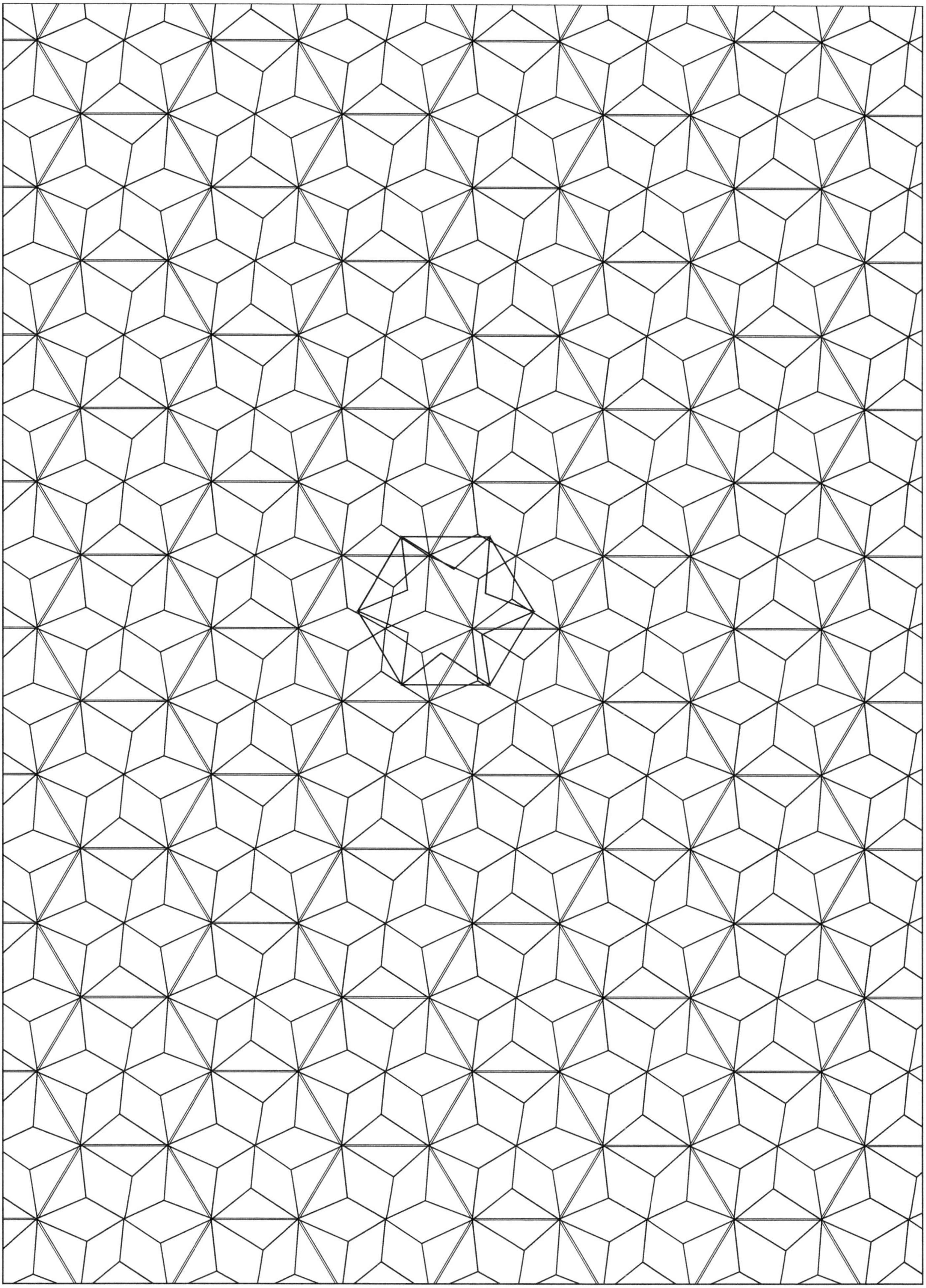

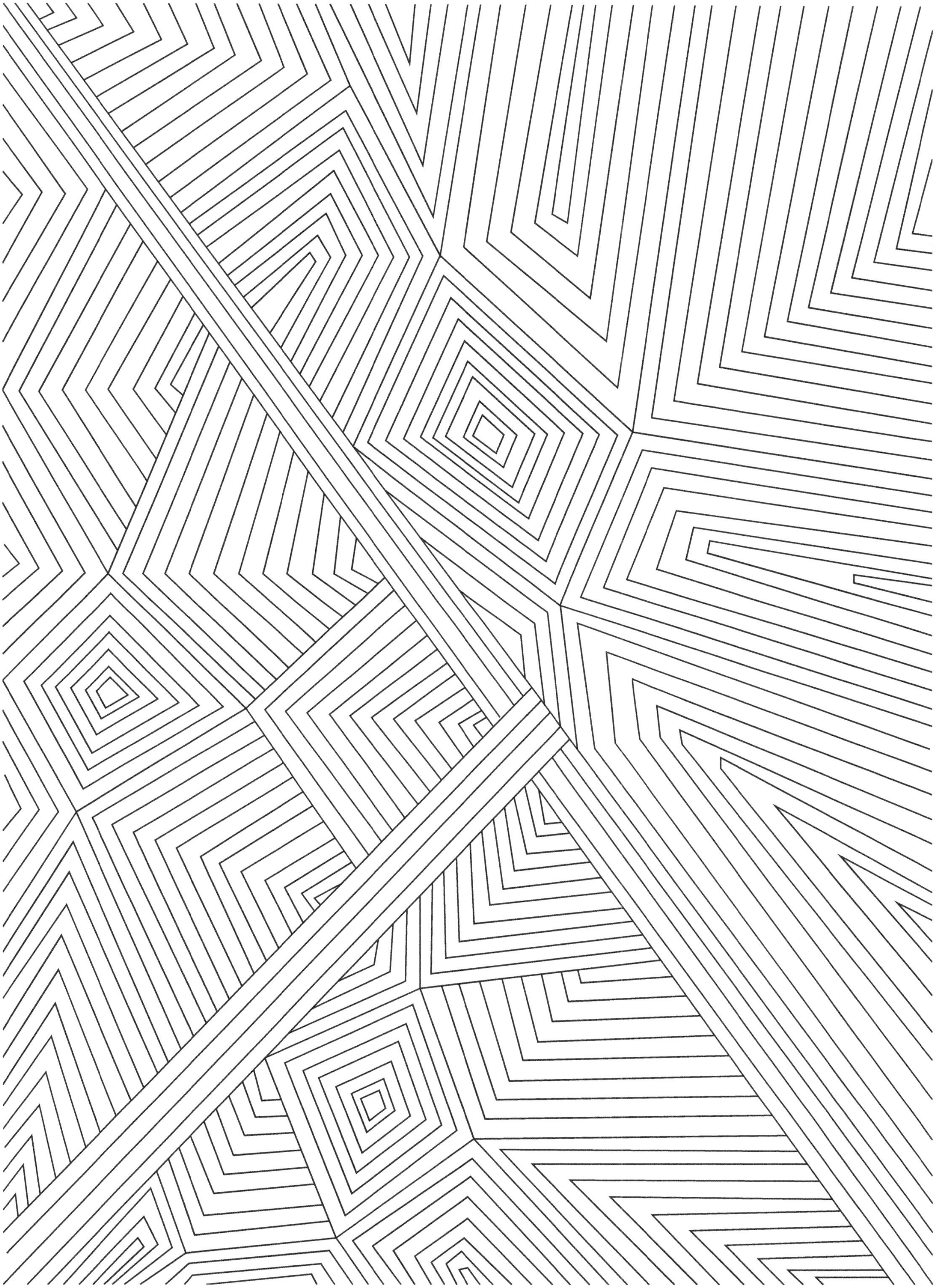

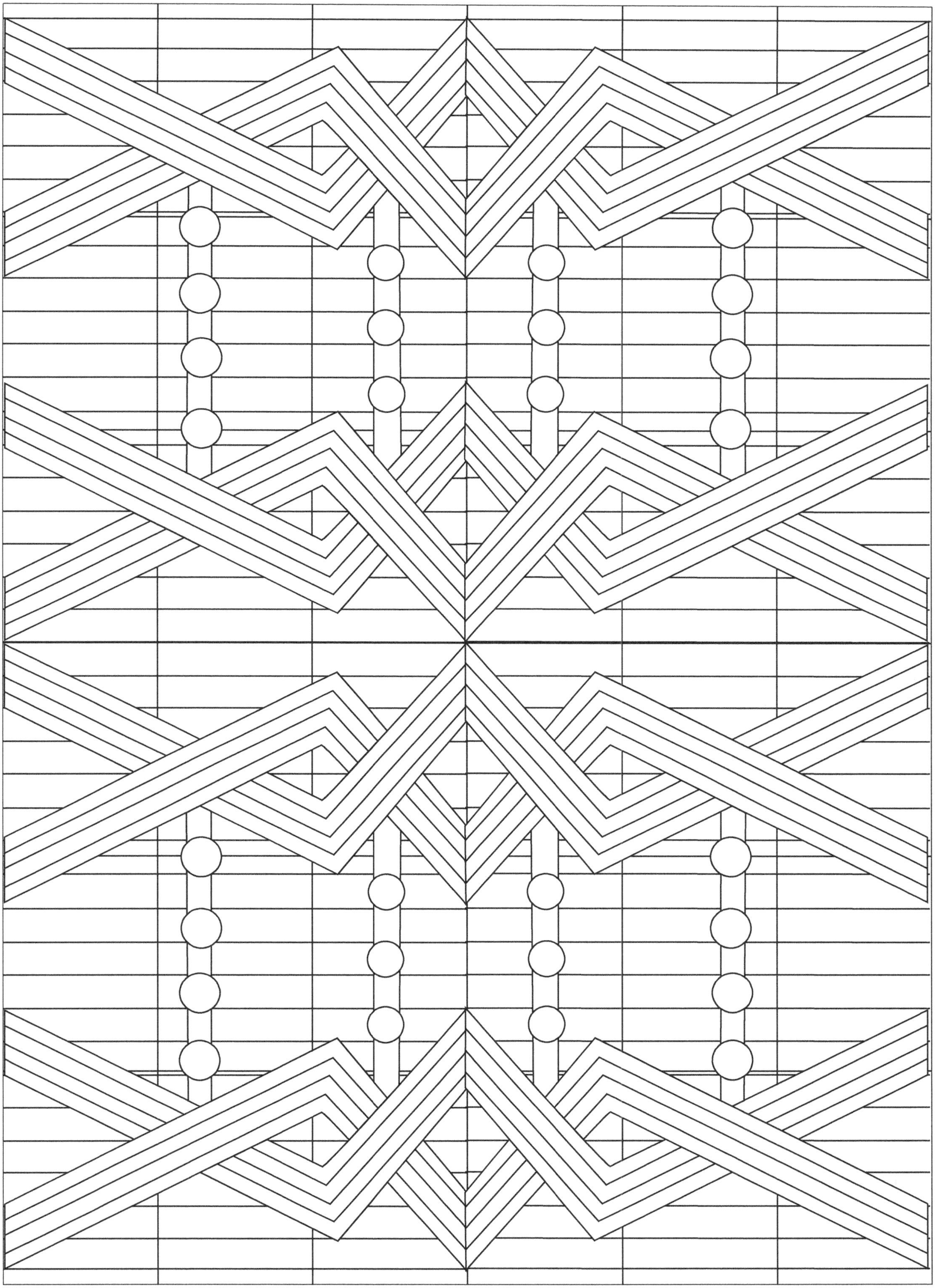

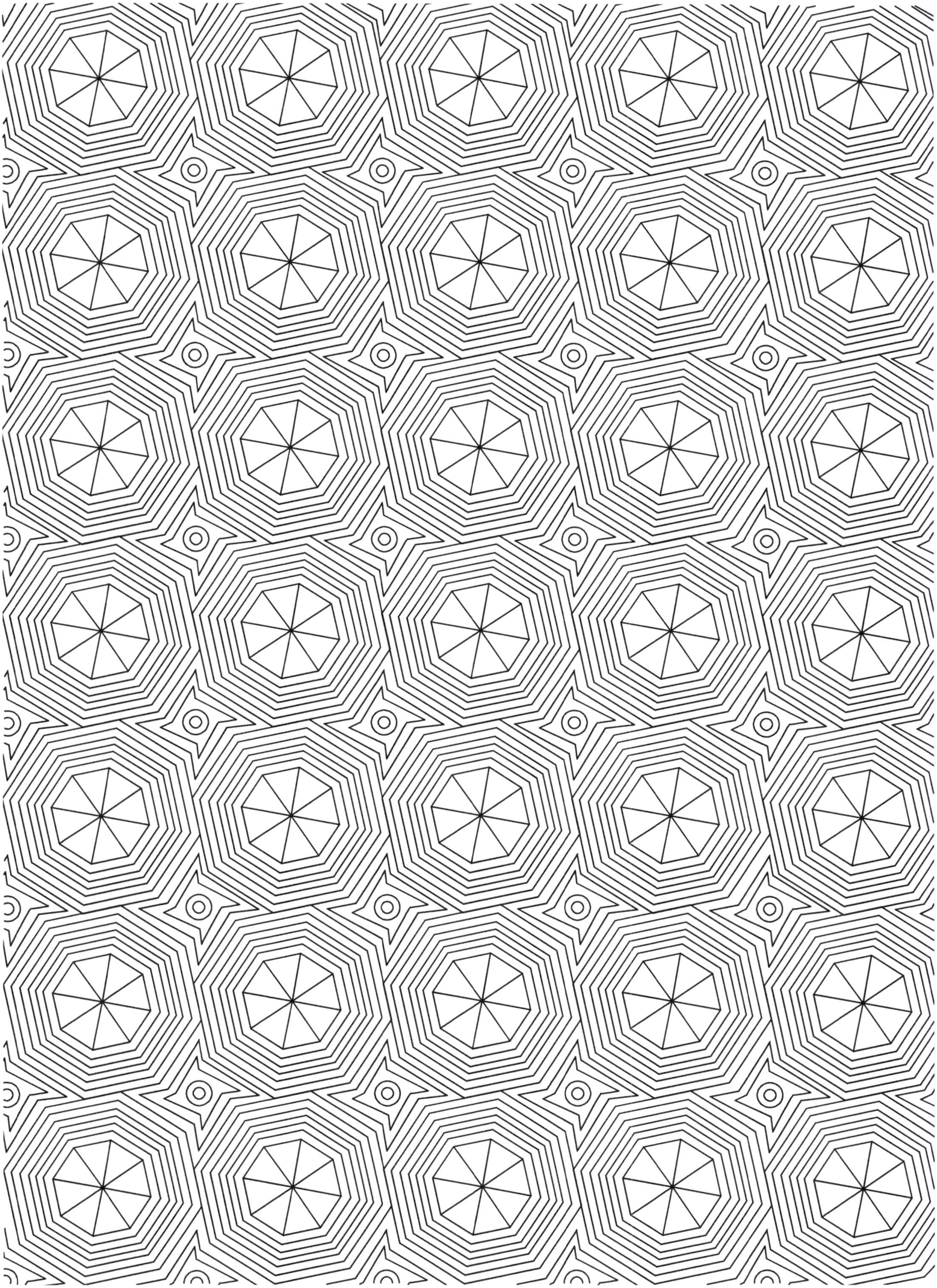

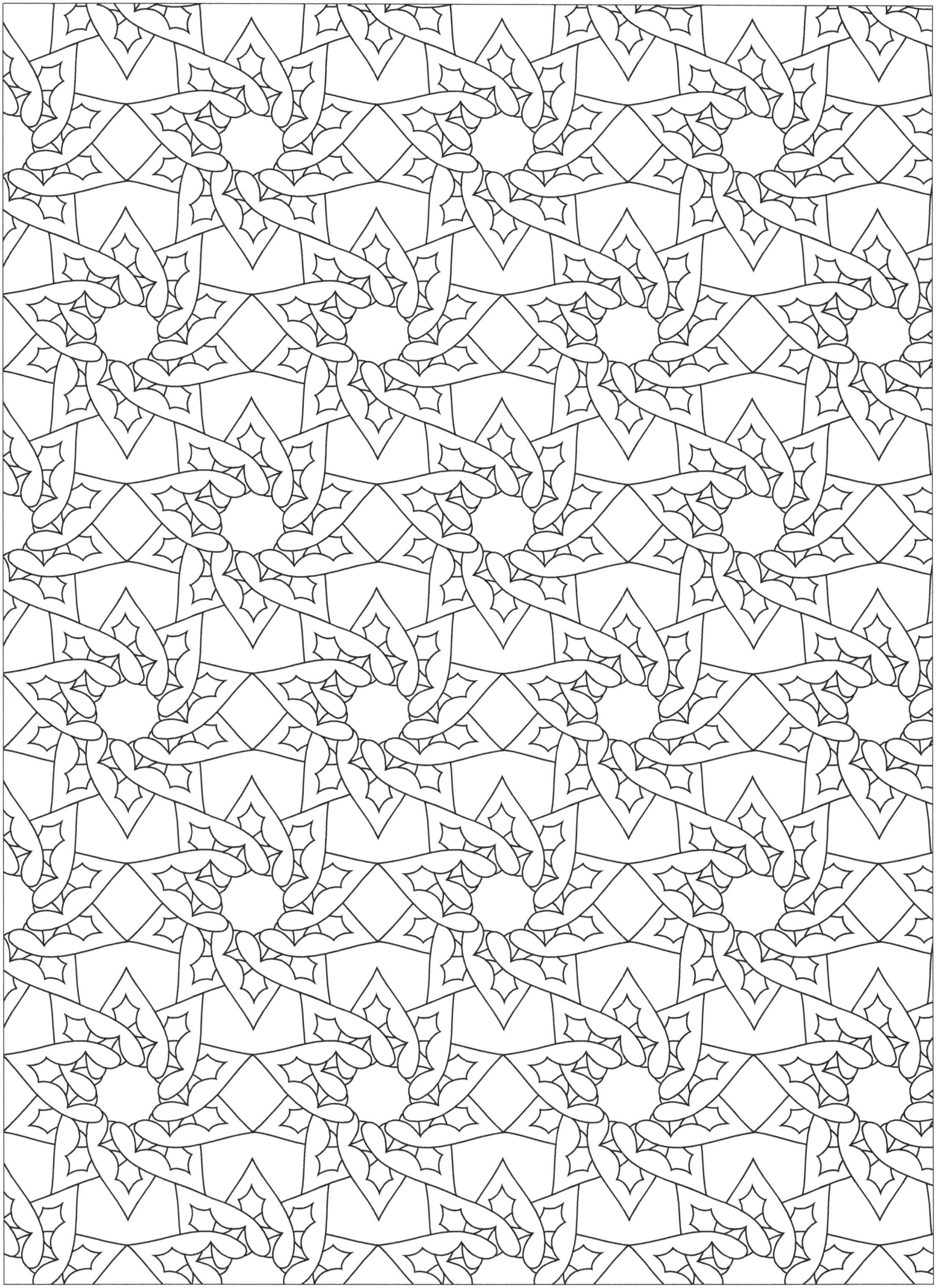

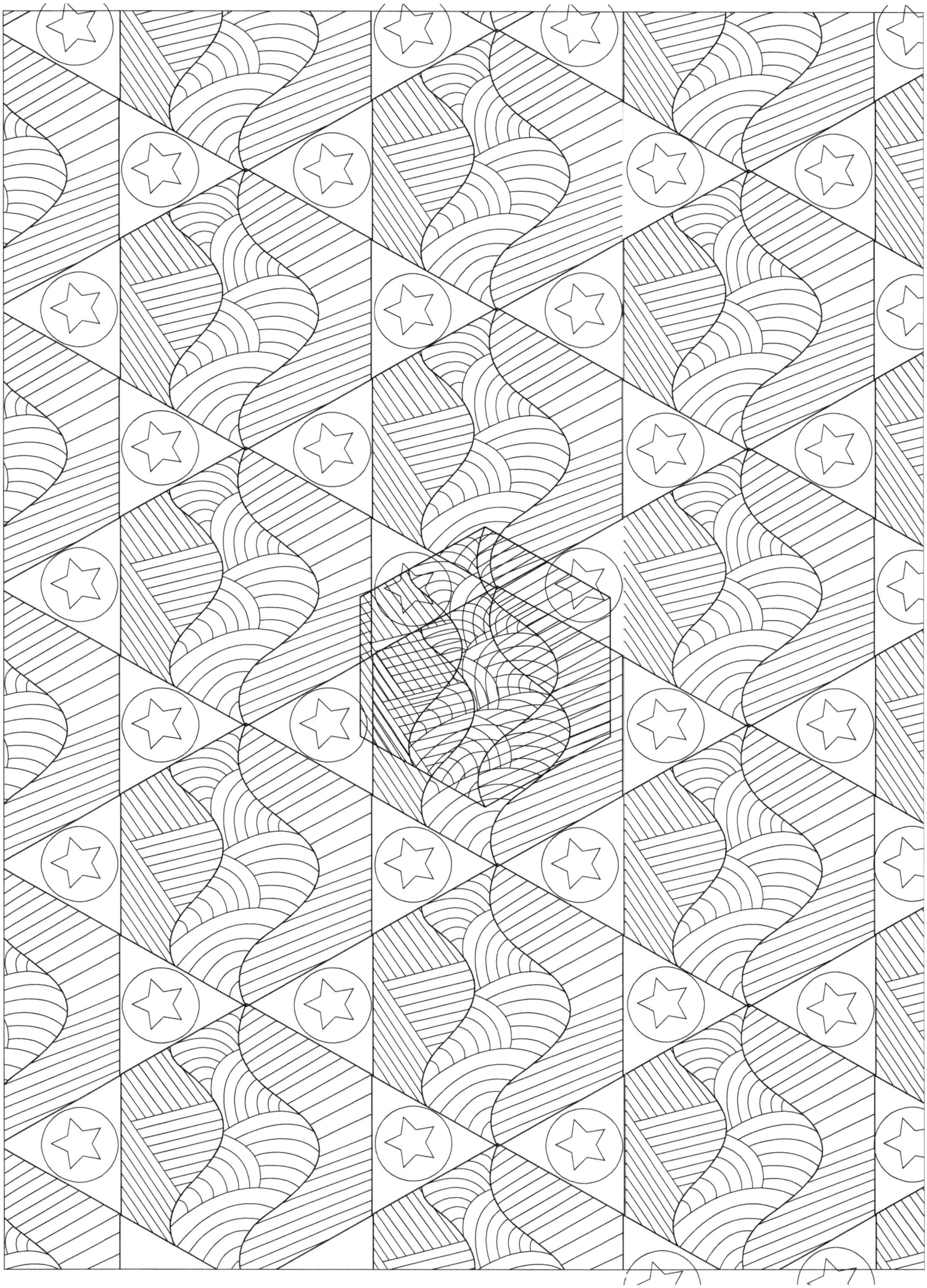

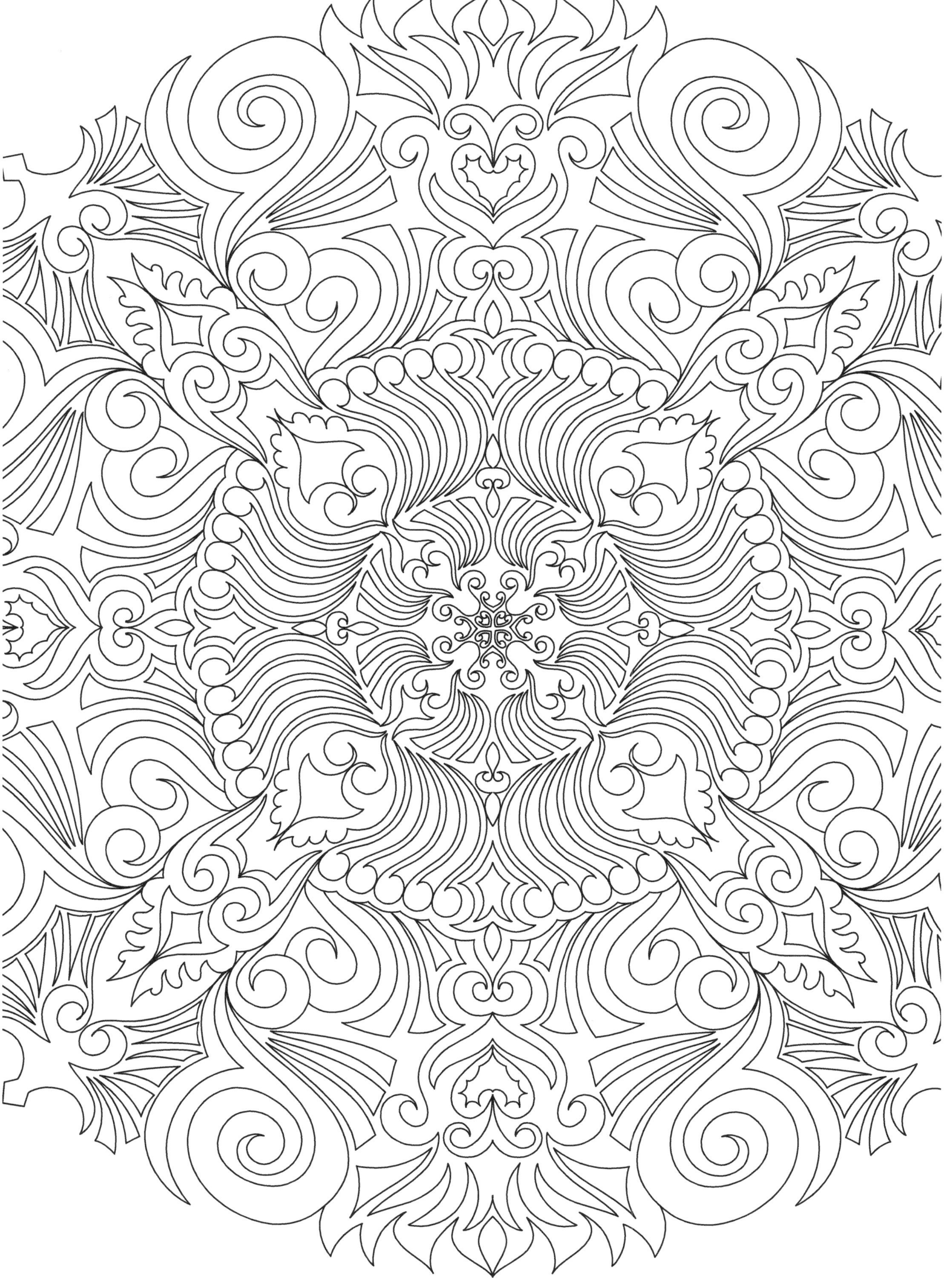

MAZE

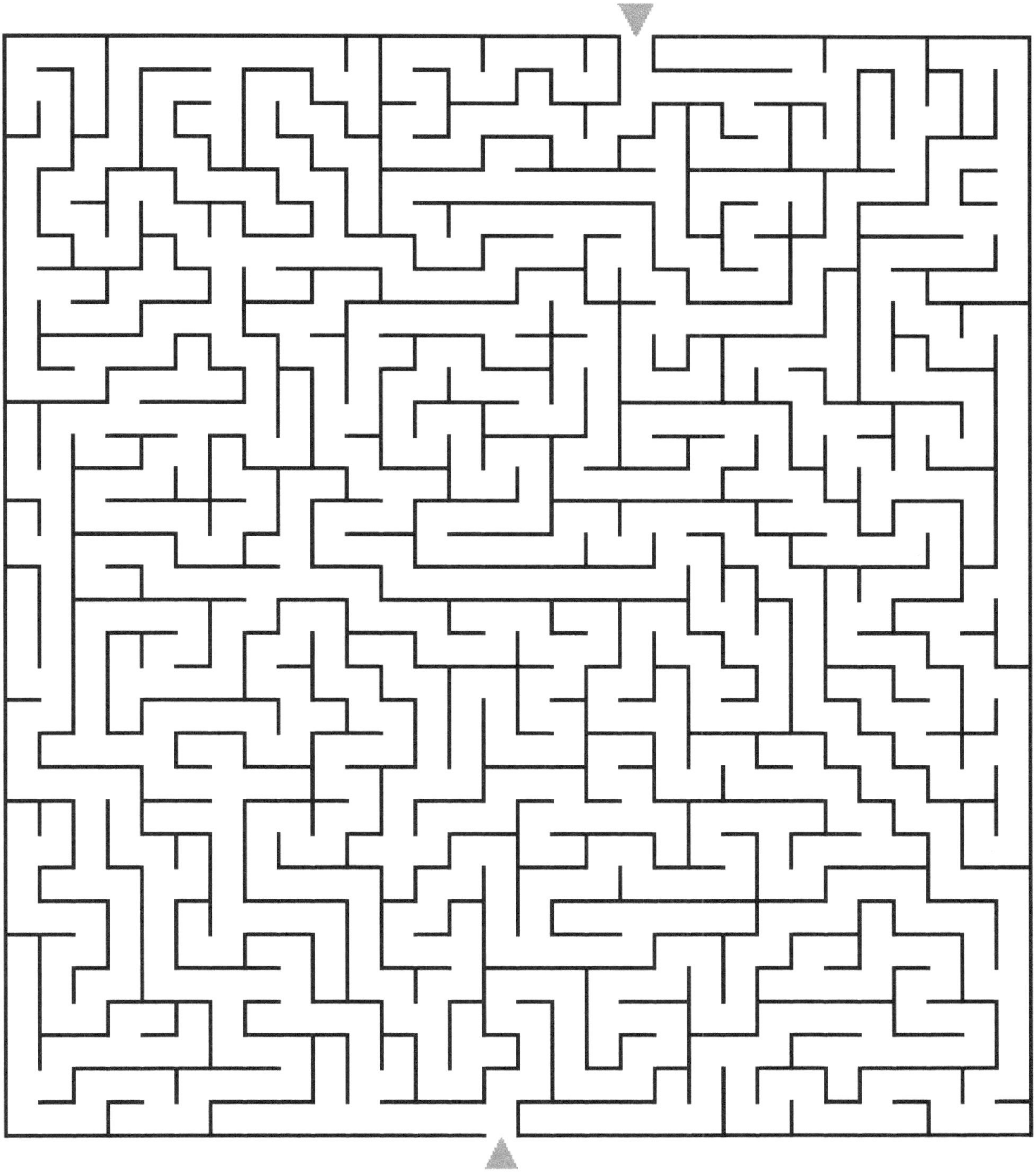

COLOR CHARTS

Solution

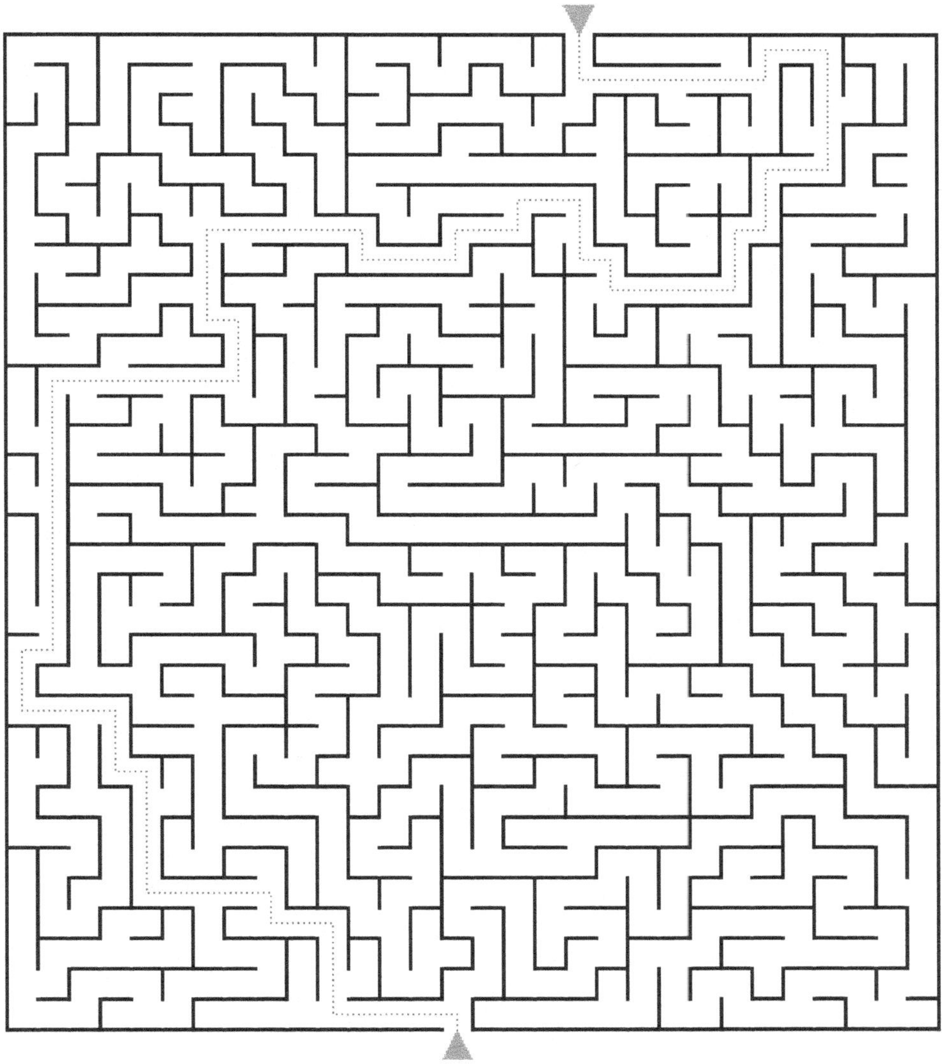

www.ingramcontent.com/pod-product-compliance
Lightning Source LLC
Chambersburg PA
CBHW081417220526
45466CB00014B/2616
* 9 7 8 1 6 9 1 2 9 3 6 7 4 *